The Past in the Past:
The Significance
of Memory and Tradition
in the Transmission of Culture

Edited by

Mercourios Georgiadis
Chrysanthi Gallou

BAR International Series 1925
2009

Published in 2016 by
BAR Publishing, Oxford

BAR International Series 1925

The Past in the Past: The Significance of Memory and Tradition in the Transmission of Culture

ISBN 978 1 4073 0407 6

BAR Publishing is the trading name of British Archaeological Reports (Oxford) Ltd.
British Archaeological Reports was first incorporated in 1974 to publish the BAR
Series, International and British. In 1992 Hadrian Books Ltd became part of the BAR
group. This volume was originally published by Archaeopress in conjunction with
British Archaeological Reports (Oxford) Ltd / Hadrian Books Ltd, the Series principal
publisher, in 2009. This present volume is published by BAR Publishing, 2016.

Printed in England

BAR
PUBLISHING

BAR titles are available from:

BAR Publishing
122 Banbury Rd, Oxford, OX2 7BP, UK
EMAIL   info@barpublishing.com
PHONE +44 (0)1865 310431
FAX   +44 (0)1865 316916
www.barpublishing.com

Contents

Introduction

Mercourios Georgiadis and Chrysanthi Gallou

The present volume is the outcome of a session held at the 12ᵗʰ European Archaeological Association conference at Krakow in Poland, in September 2006, titled *The Past in the Past: the significance of Memory and Tradition in the transmission of Culture.* In the papers presented in this session as well as in the chapters presented in this volume there were three central concepts which were very closely linked and interrelated, memory, tradition and identity. It became apparent that there were various ways in which they were perceived and consciously exploited within different societies. The purpose of this volume is to present several studies related to these issues and highlight different dimensions. The aim is not to cover all of these aspects, but to offer fresh views with up-to-date approaches on specific examples which follow different theoretical and thematic paths. The papers in this volume are chronologically diverse, covering prehistory, the classical period, the middle ages and as well as modern times, and are presented in this order. Spatially, they are concentrated in the Aegean and Scandinavia, offering different geographical contexts. The first six chapters examine how the past is used in the past, while the last two are concerned with how the past is used within present societies.

In the first chapter, Hélène Whittaker provides a valuable introduction to the meanings and the roles memory may have in any society. She then applies these aspects to the burial record and examines how memory is connected to material culture, tombs and the beliefs and practices related to burials.

The spatial and temporal period she discusses is in the mainland Greek MBA, and she attempts to follow the degree of continuity from previous periods. The issue of the 'coming of the Greeks' is examined, with a review of older hypothesis as well as new evidence. It is proposed that the changes and destructions witnessed at the end of the EBA are the result of conflicts between two peoples sharing the same landscape the agriculturalists and the nomadic or semi-nomadic pastoralists. Every day elements such as pottery styles and house plans may indicate connections with the past, while burial mounds suggest new claims over the land. The burial context was a new arena for displaying social messages such as egalitarianism, a characteristic of the nomadic way of life.

In the second chapter, Kathryn Soar focuses on Neopalatial Crete and the artistic depiction and performance of the ritual of bull-leaping. She emphasizes the hiatus between its first representation in EM II and its re-emergence some 300 years later in MM IIIB-LM IA, setting the question for the motives behind this phenomenon. The hypothesis that bull-leaping was primarily a Knossian image, exported in some cases, is examined, while the actual act of bull-leaping is believed to have taken place within the Central Court of the Palace. Soar emphasises that in EM II bull-leaping is represented in burial contexts open to all the community, whilst in the MM IIIB-LM IA period it was confined to the Palace Central Court, where the participants were specifically selected. In order to understand the meanings attributed to representations of bull-leaping, the political conditions of Neopalatial Crete are examined, and an argument for heterarchy across the island is made. Within these political entities, factions competed for social and/or political dominance, and performances are believed to have played an important role in displaying this competition. Bull leaping is considered to be a tradition invented during the Neopalatial period, which provided direct links to the past while at the same time reinventing and ascribing it with new social meanings. Thus, the bull-leaping tradition legitimised Neopalatial social conditions and emphasised the identity of the ruling class.

In the third chapter, Mercourios Georgiadis attempts to comprehend the sociopolitical conditions of East Aegean-Western Anatolia during the Late Bronze Age. In order to understand this region, the hypothesis of Mycenaean expansion into the Aegean islands and sites in Western Anatolia is presented. A short description of the sites of East Aegean-Western Anatolia with Mycenaean material is provided, highlighting the number of cemeteries recovered in this area. A rough division between North and South is drawn, with an emphasis on the northern part of the region and the character of the Mycenaean elements within the local burial contexts. It is argued that the newly introduced characteristics formed a new memory and tradition with social, political and cultural messages, which overall present an anti-Hittite ideology. In order to support this thesis, the Hittite texts are examined, in particular Hittite relations with the Mycenaeans and Western Anatolia. The anti-Hittite feeling in this region is clearly shown through a number of revolts and even a confederacy, while there are strong suggestions of Western Anatolian alliances with some of the Mycenaeans. It is suggested that the burial context was an open field for expressing these political and cultural messages, by using Mycenaean elements as an ideological manifestation.

In chapter four Melanie Wrigglesworth moves the focus from the Aegean to West Norway, and its rock art and landscape from the late Mesolithic to the Early Iron Age. She argues that, through collective memory, rock art forms social and/or cultural identities. In order to achieve this, a 'language' is used as a medium with images, full of metaphors and symbolic meanings. This expression of memory is achieved via specific places in the landscape, monuments, bodily performances and the material culture. The past, invoked through memory, is used for legitimising claims, and for this reason traditions can be constructed for this purpose. Rock art in this region is of a different style, but it is embedded into the landscape and narrates meaningful and important stories for its audience. Thus, they become centres of collective memory and consequently of group identity. The Hardanger fjord is located in western Norway and possesses a number of examples of rock art across various sites, which Wrigglesworth describes. Both their themes and their dating vary considerably, suggesting a very long period during which this area was a significant focal point. The sharing of group experience suggests that the same cultural identities were expressed through shared memories and a common past.

In the fifth chapter James Roy reviews Arkadian identity in the Classical period, a period better recorded than the previous discussions. He demonstrates the different levels of identity that coexisted during that period in Greece and Arkadia in particular. The geographical location of Arkadia in an exclusively mountainous area separates it from most Greek city-states with coastal regions. The upland population was considered by ancient and modern authors as backwards, and the land as poor. Although the landscape setting of this region had limits, Arkadia is not poorer than other areas in contemporary Greece. The archaeological finds argue that this region had the same economic and political organisation of other Greek city states. Identities at a tribal level, as well as city-state and more generic levels such as Arkadian existed and shifted over time, with more emphasis on one rather the other. The Arkadians portrayed themselves as autochthonous, occupying their territory since remote antiquity. Nonetheless, the material culture does not show them to be different from their neighbours, as testified by the imposing temples and the Megalopolis theatre.

In the sixth chapter, Pandelis Constantinakos and Metaxia Papapostolou demonstrate how the Spartan educational system of the classical period integrated girls on an equal basis to boys. In such a way, it becomes apparent that the Spartans thought of women's role in their social structure as very significant. There are many historical examples as well as historical sources used to underline such a belief. Thus, the identities of Spartan women appear to be much more complex than in other contemporary Greek city-states.

Magdalena Naum, in the seventh chapter, explores the role of memory in sustaining the cultural identity of the migrating Slavic populations in early medieval times on the Danish island of Bornholm, in the central part of the Baltic Sea. She is interested in the close link between memory, migration and cultural/ethnic identity. Remembering and forgetting are important tools for cultural memory on both an individual and a collective level. After the arrival of the migrants, some of their ritual activities changed as a result of the new conditions, while others persisted. The recovered cemeteries demonstrate an array of finds and unusual customs for this period in comparison to the rest of Denmark. These elements bear close resemblance to the northern regions where the western Slavic population resided. The most significant of the finds is the use of jewellery and other items related to dressing, which argue for a strong symbolism attributed to dress and the body by the immigrants.

In the eighth chapter Anna Simandiraki and Trevor Grimshaw review the way the material culture of the Minoan civilisation has been used in the last century. They reveal how the modern conception of this culture is projected amongst archaeologists to the public. This study is defined and treated as a discourse, which affects and modifies the way we think. Branding is another important aspect of this analysis, which characterises marketing and promoting of a product. The use of Minoan materiality in a large variety of modern produce with iconic images from this culture is presented. On a commercial level, this trend is private as much as public, while at the same time it is promoted through a number of examples as a communal Cretan identity. Additionally, the authors argue that Minoan branding can be found in academia as well. They draw our attention to how archaeology today, particularly Minoan archaeology, produces and consumes memory and tradition.

Charlotta Hillerdal in the final chapter concentrates on the link between archaeology and national identity in Sweden. The national state ideology argues for a common national origin and culture, which is expressed through a shared history. In the same context, an 'official prehistory' has been formulated by archaeologists, particularly during the 19th century. History serves the needs of the present and it is inextricably linked with tradition and identity, especially national identity. History is not just an academic subject, but an active unifying force within society between people and the past. From the 19th century there was a tendency for history to understand traditions and aspects of communality that bound people together. In the same period, and in the same socio-political context, archaeology as a discipline was developed, while cultural heritage was used for the promotion of collective memory through material remains. During this period, the Swedish identified themselves with the Vikings, clearly shown in both historical and lyrical works. Although the Viking Age is a wider Scandinavian phenomenon, different aspects of it are highlighted in Norway and Sweden. The national ideology promoted homogenisation, and history and archaeology have contributed to that by offering a common origin, ancestry and authenticity.

From these summaries, it soon becomes apparent that there are many different aspects to the recognition of memory, tradition and identity and the ways in which they are interlinked. More specifically, it is suggested in the opening chapter that remembering and forgetting can be equally used to either promote or hinder older traditions according to new socio-cultural conditions. In the second chapter, we see an example of the selection of an older tradition in forging a connection with the past in order to promote new social conditions with altered social messages. In the third chapter the newly introduced tradition is more or less contemporary, and represents ideological manifestations with clear political and cultural messages. The fourth chapter focuses on the long continuity of rock art as a focal point, and the use of memory and the past for expressing shared cultural identities. In the fifth chapter the focus is on the perceived and projected past in the formation of ethnic identities, while the material record argues differently. In the sixth chapter it becomes clear how education provided equal opportunities for both boys and girls, as well as varied social identities for the latter varied social identities. The seventh chapter emphasises the role of memory in the cultural/ethnic identity of migratory populations, and how this is expressed within a specific burial context. The eighth chapter addresses the issue of archaeology in the formation of modern memories and traditions on several levels, such as the commercial, social and academic. In the final chapter the role of history and archaeology is assessed in forming national identities, by providing a homogenised historical memory and a narrative with a common origin and ancestry. We hope that this volume will advance discussions and studies related to memory, tradition and identity in order to better understand the past, either in the past or in the present.

Memory and Cultural Values in the Middle Helladic Period
Some Preliminary Thoughts

Helène Whittaker

Memory connects the present with the past on individual and collective levels and plays an important role in all societies. On a collective level memories of the past are often inextricably associated with the definition of cultural or ethnic identity and origins. Communal memory holds societies together and is bound up with social and political organisation. In most societies the past is, to a greater or lesser extent, considered normative. A major function of memory is therefore to ensure that the values and beliefs associated with the past continue to maintain their force. What societies choose to remember and how they do it is a consequence of their social and moral world-view (Connerton 1989; Halbwachs 1992).

Memory of the past can be preserved by written accounts, in the oral tradition, and through performance, for instance in commemorative ceremonies, which may be re-enactments of past events, or in ritual activity (Connerton 1989, 39). In many societies certain people, such as religious specialists or epic singers, are entrusted with remembrance on behalf of the community (Clanchy 1970, 168-70; Howell 1991, 233). However, there is a sense in which memory needs matter, and the conveying and preservation of the past is often also associated with materiality (Renfrew 2004, 28; Jones 2007). The materialisation of memory ensures that past continues to be visible and therefore also to affect the lives of the living in a particularly efficacious way.

The significance of material culture in this regard is also related to the fact that objects often have longer life-spans than human beings. It can furthermore be argued that in pre- and proto-historical societies material culture plays a more overt role as the conveyor of ideas and concepts which derive their force from the past than was or is the case in societies in which writing is known and in relatively common use (Bradley 2002). The association between the need or the desire to preserve the past and material culture is obvious in the case of burial markers or large public monuments which are explicitly constructed for the transmission of memories between generations. The significance and power of heirloom objects which are regarded as valuable and passed down from generation to generation precisely because they are associated with the memory of particular events and particular individuals have often been discussed in various cultural contexts (Lillios 1999; Härke 2000; Williams 2006, 40-1). However, all forms of material culture can embody memories of the past, albeit in less obvious or specific ways (Hoskins 1998, 50; Moreland 2001, 80-4). Domestic architecture, for example, or the various items used in daily life may reflect the social and symbolic importance of maintaining ties to the past.

In the Middle Helladic period the general lack of evidence for material ostentation, ritual elaboration, and extensive trading contacts has usually been interpreted in terms of poverty, cultural backwardness, and isolation.

However, other perspectives may also be valid to understanding the culture and society of the Middle Helladic period. For instance, the fact that cross-cultural evidence indicates that societies where maintaining the values and beliefs associated with the past and the lifestyle of the ancestors is considered crucial to the well-being of the living are often also hostile to innovation, material ostentation, and foreign influence could be taken into account (Bloch 1971; Andersen 1998). It could then be questioned whether the apparent material poverty and backwardness of the Greek mainland in the Middle Bronze Age is to be interpreted entirely in terms of deprivation, or if it could, in part at least, be understood as the reflection of a world view which was determined to a significant extent by memories of an earlier way of life and the values and beliefs associated with it.

That this last might be the case is suggested by the artificial mounds or tumuli which constitute a characteristic feature of the Middle Helladic period. These tumuli were with a few exceptions used for multiple burials. Their monumentality and visibility in the landscape strongly suggest that relations with the dead played a structuring role in Middle Helladic society (Müller 1989; Cavanagh and Mee 1998; Hielte 2004, 27-8; Borgna and Càssola Guida 2007; Whittaker forthcoming). It is, however, noteworthy that in several cases the construction of a tumulus would seem unrelated to any funerary purpose. This was the case with the earliest examples at Lerna (Caskey 1955; 1956) and at Olympia (Kyrieleis 1990; 2006; Rambach 2002, 194) which date to the end of the Early Helladic II period. It can therefore be suggested that the tumulus mounds were in themselves important symbols which invested the landscape with meaning (Whittaker, forthcoming). Furthermore, it is notable that in several cases a tumulus is built over the remains of earlier habitation or

the fill of the mound incorporates sherds and other material associated with human activity which must have been taken from a deserted or destroyed settlement in the vicinity. This is the case at Ayios Iannis-Papoulia, Routsi-Myrsinochorion (Korres 1993, 231-48), Voidokoilia (Korres 1978), Lerna (Caskey 1955, 32-5; 1956, 155-7, 165-6), Corinth (Rutter 1990), and Thebes (Spyropoulos 1981, 102). This reuse of earlier habitation can be interpreted as an act of remembrance, where the intention must have been to establish links in a very visible manner with those who in previous times had inhabited the same landscapes. It would seem very possible then that the tumuli functioned as important loci of social memory which were associated with myths of origins and with life in a long-lost and idealised past. Ideas about the ancestors and their way of life may therefore have been important to the developments which took place after the collapse of Early Helladic II social organisation and may have continued to inform the world view of the inhabitants of the Greek mainland throughout the greater part of the Middle Helladic period. The way of life led by the inhabitants of the Greek mainland during the Early Bronze Age, and the nature of the transition between the Early and the Middle Bronze Ages, may be of greater significance to an understanding of Middle Helladic culture than has been generally recognised.

The Early Helladic II period, which was characterised by a distinctive material culture and a complex and hierarchical social organisation, came to an end for reasons which are still unclear. A series of destructions throughout the central Greek area indicates that it was followed by a lengthy period of widespread unrest. These destructions have traditionally been associated with the invasions of new peoples who spoke an Indo-European language and who can be recognised as the ancestors of the later Greeks. Their advent was believed to have changed the culture of Bronze Age Greece in fundamental ways (Blegen 1928;

Haley 1928; Caskey 1960, 299-303). This was a view of events which presented itself as tempting and almost self-evident after the decipherment of Linear B revealed that Greek was the administrative language of the Mycenaean palaces. It was believed (or assumed) that the pre-existing inhabitants of the Greek mainland were, if not totally exterminated, at least culturally submerged by the less advanced but more aggressive culture of the newcomers.

However, as has been well-recognised, there are a number of problems associated with this scenario. The Indo-European tribes are often envisaged as nomadic warriors and this is reflected (implicitly or explicitly) in the common characterisation of the later Mycenaean culture as singularly warlike (see, for example Kristiansen 2005). It is strange therefore that evidence for warfare as well as for the social and symbolic importance of warrior ideology is conspicuously absent in the material culture of the Middle Helladic period. More significantly, as Forsén has shown, the destructions seemingly occur at various times and places throughout the Early Helladic II and III periods (Forsén 1992). New types of artefacts also appear at different times in different places (Forsén 1992; Maran 1998, 3-4; Rutter 2001, 114-5). Accordingly, it is not possible to map out the progress of an invading new people down into central and southern Greek from areas to the north. Weiberg (2007, 100-1, 180-1) has pointed out that accidental fires which spread rapidly or deliberate demolition by the original inhabitants themselves could, in a number of cases including the House of the Tiles at Lerna, constitute alternative explanations for the destructions. The extent of the burning at Lerna is not known (Forsén 1992, 33, 158; Maran 1998, 162).

However, it must be significant in some way that the archaeological evidence indicates that at many sites the Early Helladic III period represents a radical break in material culture (Manning 1997, 150-1; Maran 1998, 204, 222, 278). At all sites where both Early Helladic II and III levels have been recognised there is a marked discontinuity in architecture, ceramics, and social organisation as has been emphasised by Maran (1998, 222). By the time of the beginning of the Middle Helladic period it can be said that a new social order has been established, which presents a stark contrast to the elaborateness and sophistication of the Early Helladic II period. Although most Aegean scholars are now unhappy with the "coming of the Greeks" hypothesis, the idea that this change is in some way to be explained in ethnic terms as the arrival of new people with a different culture is difficult to scrap entirely.

As an alternative to the idea of invading tribes, it would seem possible to propose that the fact that the destructions which characterise the end of the Early Helladic II and the Early Helladic III periods do not conform to any pattern of time or space indicates that they were caused by people who were already present in central and southern Greece. It can be suggested that violent conflicts between two different groups of people who were sharing the same landscape, or perhaps rather different parts of it, caused or constituted a significant factor in the collapse of Early Helladic II culture. Ethnographic evidence for more that one group of people with very different lifestyles living in the same area is plentiful. It is also not difficult to find examples which indicate that interaction may be at best precarious, characterised by mutual suspicion which can become murderous if disturbed (Håland 1969; Sherratt 1981, 289; Khazanov 1983, 35-7; Okely 1983; Lewis 1987, 12; Hielte 2004). Conflict between nomads and settled farmers over land and natural resources is, for example, an important factor in the ongoing tragedy in Darfur (Ahmed and Manger 2006). With regard to prehistoric Greece Hielte (2004) has argued that nomadic lifestyles could have existed throughout prehistory. Her focus was on the Middle Helladic period, but the idea that a significant segment of the population could have lived in a nomadic or semi-nomadic fashion during the greater part of the Early Helladic period would seem equally probable. As emphasised by Hielte nomadic populations have lived in the Greek landscape up until modern times. If this was the case, it could further be suggested that towards the end of the Early Helladic II period the traditional relationship between settled agriculturalists and pastoralists deteriorated resulting in the destruction of settlements and the displacement of people.

As already mentioned, from the end of the Early Helladic II period there is a clear association between the construction of tumulus mounds and earlier settlement. It would seem possible that the particular importance of materialising ties with previous populations at this time should be seen as a reflection a strong necessity to mark territorial rights. The tumulus mounds could be said to anchor the people associated with them to the land. This could be an indication that control of land and access to natural resources had become a source of conflict, possibly as a result of environmental changes which could have led to increasing sedentarisation among previously more mobile populations. It may be relevant that climate change seems to have been a factor in the collapse of political and social organisation and changes in settlement patterns which are taking place in various areas of the eastern Mediterranean towards the end of the third millennium (Courty and Weiss 1997; Hassan 1997; Hole 1997, 52-6; Rosen 1997; Hielte 2004, 33). It is, however, difficult to see all these as related and due to a common cause, and moreover the evidence for climate change on the Greek mainland seems inconclusive (Manning 1997). It would seem significant, however, that in the later part of Early Helladic II an alluvium deposit in the Argolid occurs after a long period of ground stability. It is believed to be the result of erosion caused by human activity but it may also have been related also to changes in the climate (van Andel and

Runnels 1987, 92; Pullen 1992, 47; Jameson et al. 1994, 182-94; Manning 1997, 152; Maran 1998, 255-9). The result was the loss of usable agricultural land, and this could have affected the lives of nomadic populations as well as of settled agriculturalists, and not only in the Argolid.

Direct evidence for the existence of a sizeable nomadic or semi-nomadic population is hard to find in Early Helladic Greece. This is not surprising as it is in the nature of people who are constantly on the move to leave few material remains (Smith 2005, 44-50). Furthermore, with regard to the periods following on from the Neolithic and the beginnings of sedentary life, archaeological interest in Europe has been mainly focused on farmers (Zvelebil 1996; Hielte 2004, 55). However, there is some evidence from the Greek Early Bronze Age which can be mentioned in this connection. Dickinson (1994, 37) has suggested that in the later Neolithic pastoralist groups developed, who would have interacted through trade with the settled agricultural population. The possibility that there may have been an increased reliance on pastoral production in the Early Helladic period has been commented on by several scholars (Wiencke 1989, 500; Whitelaw 2000, 145). A number of upland sites which were in use during the Early Bronze Age may be associated with pastoralism (Halstead 1981, 326; 2000, 118; Barker 2005, 55). The fact that bone evidence indicates that the number of sheep increases in the Early Bronze Age could possibly be a reflection of the development of herding as a separate occupation from agriculture (Sherratt 1981, 283). In particular, it could be argued that the widespread use of caves from the later Neolithic could have been used as short-time shelters by pastoralists (Halstead 2000, 118). On the other hand, the fact that caves were used for a variety of purposes in later prehistory weakens the hypothesis that the evidence for human activity in caves in the Neolithic and Early Bronze Age is necessarily to be associated with some form of herding, as has been pointed out by Halstead (2000, 118). He thinks it likely that there was no specialised pastoralism during the Bronze Age (Halstead 2000, 122). Mee (2001, 10) has pointed out that in Early Helladic Laconia there appears to be two different settlement patterns, with nucleated settlements in the lowlands and more dispersed habitation in the highlands. He suggests that they are to be associated with different types of agricultural practice, and perhaps also with pastoralism. In any case, the settlement pattern in Laconia can be said to provide some support for the idea that different groups with differing ways of life could have coexisted in parts of the Greek mainland during the Early Bronze Age. Consequently, it may be possible to hypothesise that in addition to the settled agriculturalists, who were responsible for what we think of as Early Helladic II culture, there also existed a more nomadic people whose presence in the landscape has left few discernable archaeological traces. The diverse ways of life followed by different groups could through time have developed into separate identities which may have been conceived in cultural or ethnic terms.

In the Early Helladic III period features which are already present in the Greek area taken as a whole, start to show up in new places. For instance, Rutter (1982; 1995, 479-623) has argued that the Early Helladic III pottery from Lerna shows influence from the so-called Lefkandi ware which was in use in central Greece already in the Early Helladic II period. The apsidal house form has traditionally been seen as evidence for the arrival of new people. However, Forsén (1992, 197-203; Maran 1998, 199-201) has pointed out that they also occur in the Early Helladic II period in the central Greek area. There are possible examples from the Peloponnese as well as from Thebes and Pefkakia-Magoula, and they seem to have a long tradition in Thessaly. Apsidal houses should accordingly be regarded as a feature which becomes more popular from the Early

Helladic period onwards rather than as an innovation. Influences from the west Balkans and the central Mediterranean, which seem to be a new development in the Early Helladic III period, have been discussed in detail by Maran (1998; 2007) who suggests the possibility that movement of people from the northwestern Balkans to western Greece. It would seem possible that the fact that influences from central Greece, the Cetina-culture of the northwestern coast of the Balkans and from the east Aegean appear in the northeast Peloponnese in the Early Helladic III period could be explained in terms of the increasing sedentism of people who had been used to moving around over a fairly extensive area.

Rutter (1988, 88, n.9; 1995, 479-595) suggests that the forms and decorative elements of the pattern-painted pottery found at Lerna were derived from basketry, while the central Greek light-on-dark type may imitate gourds. As he points out, the imitation of basketry and gourds could represent a reference to a nomadic lifestyle which primarily used baskets and hollowed gourds rather than ceramic vessels as containers (Rutter 1988, 85-6; Hielte 2004, 59). The imitation in more permanent materials of artefacts which were originally made of lighter and more portable materials can be interpreted as the wish to preserve the memories of a past or disappearing way of life. Hielte (2004, 35) has suggested that it is possible that the apsidal house form can be understood as an imitation of tents in stone and mud-brick. Consequently, it would seem possible that the most common house form may also deliberately have referred to a past way of life. It could perhaps be said that from the end of the Early Helladic II period on the one hand, the construction of tumulus mounds represents a new emphasis on territoriality and on materialising bonds with the land; on the other, references to a past way of life are intensified by being embodied in material culture, perhaps precisely because it is in the process of disappearing.

It can be suggested that after the dissolution of the social and political organisation which characterised the Early Helladic II period, many of the values which were originally associated with a nomadic and more marginal lifestyle came to dominate culturally and socially and that this laid the foundations for the development of Middle Helladic society characterised by a more or less homogenous cultural complex. From this perspective, the transition from the Early to the Middle Bronze Age on the Greek mainland can be understood as a fundamental shift in mentality. If this is the case, many aspects of Middle Helladic society can be understood in a more positive way than has often been the case. The social and political organisation of the Middle Helladic period would seem quite certainly to be less complex than that of the Early Helladic II period. This could possibly be seen as related to the fact that nomadic groups tend towards a more egalitarian social organisation with relatively little social and economic differentiation in comparison with settled societies (Khazanov 1983, 152-64). The use of tumuli for burial could be seen as related to the importance given to the dead in many nomadic societies, where a sense of family and belonging is at the centre of individual identity (Lancaster and Lancaster 1998, 27; Smith 2005, 108-11). It has been suggested here that the tumulus mounds materialised beliefs concerning the relationship between the inhabitants of the Greek mainland in the Middle Helladic period and the land in which they lived and died. It would seem possible that they were also associated with important communal rituals (Hielte 2001; Whittaker forthcoming). If this was the case, values associated with memories of the past may have been validated by religious beliefs and constantly reinforced through ritual activity. This could provide some explanation for the absence of direct evidence for religious elaboration during the Middle Helladic period. The nomadic way of life does not encourage the accumulation of material possessions (Khazanov 1998, 9; Smith 2005, 31-44). While there may be high investment

in goods which are easily portable, cross-cultural studies of nomadic populations indicate that the accumulation of material wealth as such is often associated with immorality (Okely 1983, 64; Lancaster and Lancaster 1998, 31; Smith 2005, 31). The lack of interest in the material display of wealth, status, or power during the Middle Helladic period could therefore be understood in terms of a traditional system of values which does not associate status and authority with the possession of material goods.

In nomadic societies, important social and moral values tend to be immaterial rather than material. Hielte (2004, 56-7; Lancaster and Lancaster 1998, 27) has pointed out that freedom is highly valued by nomadic populations and that there is also an emphasis on achieving and maintaining respect and honour. Furthermore, hospitality plays an important role in reinforcing social relationships. These values may be expressed through material culture and it should therefore be possible to discuss their significance in archaeological terms. It would seem evident that the various aspects of artefacts such as form, decoration, function may have their origin in the desire to perpetuate memory. For instance, it can be suggested that the carinated forms and highly polished surfaces of Grey Minyan Ware, where vessels used for drinking or mixing liquids predominate, can be said to exhibit a very definite aesthetic consciousness which it may be possible to relate to the cultural importance of hospitality in the Middle Helladic period, an importance derived from memories of what life was like in the past (French 1973; Zerner 1993, 43).

To conclude, it can be proposed that the absence of a complex political and social organisation and the apparent lack of interest in the accumulation of material wealth which seems to characterise the greater part of the Middle Helladic period should be seen as reflecting the continued social significance of the values associated with memories of a long past and idealised way of life. The importance of the past in the Middle Helladic present provided immunity against cultural influences from the Cyclades or Crete and had a constraining effect on social change.

References

Ahmed, A.G.M. and Manger, L., (eds.) 2006. *Understanding the Crisis in Darfur. Listening to Sudanese Voices*, Bergen, University of Bergen.

Andersen, K., 1998. 'Synlig og usynlig religion: Egalitet og hierarki i Nordghana', *Religion og materiel kultur*, L. Bredholt Christensen and S.B. Sveen (eds.), Aarhus, 25-43.

Barker, G., 2005. 'Agriculture, Pastoralism, and Mediterranean Landscapes in Prehistory', *The Archaeology of Mediterranean Prehistory*, E. Blake and A. B. Knapp (eds.), Oxford, 46-76.

Blegen, C.W., 1928. 'The Coming of the Greeks: II. The Geographical Distribution of Prehistoric Remains in Greece', *American Journal of Archaeology* 32, 146-154.

Bloch, M., 1971. *Placing the Dead. Tombs, Ancestral Villages, and Kinship Organization in Madagascar*, London.

Bergna, E. and Càssola Guida, P., 2007. 'At the Fringe of the Tumulus Culture: Bronze Age Tumuli of North-Eastern Italy between Europe and the Aegean', *Between the Aegean and Baltic Seas. Prehistory across Borders*, I. Galanaki, H. Tomas, Y. Galanakis and R. Laffineur (eds.), [Aegaeum 27], Liège, 191-201.

Bradley, R., 2002. *The Past in Prehistoric Societies*, London.

Caskey, J., 1955. 'Excavations at Lerna: 1954', *Hesperia* 24, 25-49.

Caskey, J., 1956. 'Excavations at Lerna: 1955', *Hesperia* 25, 147-173.

Caskey, J., 1960. 'The Early Period in the Argolid', *Hesperia* 29, 285-303.

Cavanagh, W. and Mee, C., 1998. *A Private Place: Death in Prehistoric Greece*, [SIMA 125], Göteborg.

Clanchy, M.T., 1970. 'Remembering the Past and the Good Old Law', *History* 55, 165-176.

Connerton, P., 1989. *How Societies Remember*, Cambridge.

Courty, M.-A. and Weiss, H., 1997. 'The Scenario of Environmental Degradation in the Tell Leilan Region, Ne Syria, during the Late Third Millenium Abrupt Climate Change', *Third Millennium BC Climate Change and Old World Collapse*, H. Nüzhet Dalfes, G. Kukla and H. Weiss (eds.), Berlin, 107-147.

Dickinson, O.T.P.K., 1994. *The Aegean Bronze Age*, Cambridge.

Forsén, J., 1992. *The Twilight of the Early Helladics. A Study of the Disturbances in East-Central and Southern Greece towards the End of the Early Bronze Age*, Göteborg.

French, D.H., 1973. 'Migrations and 'Minyan' Pottery in Western Anatolia and the Aegean', *Bronze Age Migrations in the Aegean, Archaeological and Linguistic Problems in Greek Prehistory*, R. A. Crossland and A. Birchall (eds.), London, 51-7.

Haaland, G., 1969. 'Economic Determinants in Ethnic Processes', *Ethnic Groups and Boundaries. The Social organization of Culture Difference*, F. Barth (ed.), Prospect Heights, 58-134

Halbwachs, M., 1992. *On Collective Memory* (Edited, Translated, and with an Introduction by L. A. Coser), Chicago.

Haley, J.B. 1928. 'The Coming of the Greeks: I. The Geographical Distribution of Pre-Greek Place-Names', *American Journal of Archaeology* 32, 141-5.

Halstead, P., 1981. 'Counting Sheep in Neolithic and Bronze Age Grece', *Pattern of the Past. Studies in Honour of David Clarke*, I. Hodder, G. Isaac and N. Hammond (eds.), Cambridge, 307-39.

Halstead, P., 1987. 'Traditional and Ancient Rural Economy in Mediterranean Europe: Plus ça change?', *Journal of Hellenic Studies* 107, 77-87.

Halstead, P., 2000. 'Land Use in Postglacial Greece: Cultural Causes and Environmental Effects', *Landscape and Land Use in Postglacial Greece*, P. Halstead and C. Fredrick (eds.), Sheffield, 110-128.

Härke, H., 2000. 'The Circulation of Weapons in Anglo-Saxon Society', *Rituals of Power form Late Antiquity to the Early Middle Ages*, F. Theuws and J. L. Nelson (eds.), Leiden, 377-99.

Hassan, F., 1997. 'Nile Floods and Political Disorder in Early Egypt', *Third Millennium BC Climate Change and Old World Collapse*, H. Nüzhet Dalfes, G. Kukla and H. Weiss (eds.), Berlin, 1-23.

Hielte, M., 2001. 'The Horseshoe-shaped and Other Installations for Performing Rituals in Funeral Contexts in Middle Helladic and Early Mycenaean Times', *Potnia. Deities and Religion in the Aegean Bronze Age*, R. Laffineur and R. Hägg (eds.), [Aegaeum 22], Liège, 103-112.

Hielte, M., 2004. 'Sedentary versus Nomadic Lifestyles. The 'Middle Helladic People' in Southern Balkan (Late 3rd & First Half of the 2nd Millennium BC)', *Acta Archaeologica* 75, 27-94.

Hole, F., 1997. 'Evidence for Mid-Holocene Environmental Change in the Western Khabur Drainage, Northeastern Syria', *Third Millennium BC Climate Change and Old World Collapse*, H. Nüzhet Dalfes, G. Kukla and H. Weiss (eds.), Berlin, 39-66.

Hoskins, J., 1998. *Biographical Objects. How Things Tell Stories of People's Lives*, New York and London.

Howell, S., 1991. 'Access to the Ancestors. Re-contructions of the Past in Non-literate Society', *The Ecology of Choice and Symbol. Essays in Honour of Fredrik Barth*, R. Grønhaug, G. Haaland and G. Henriksen (eds.), Bergen, 225-43.

Jameson, M.H., Runnels, C.N. and van Andel, T., 1994. *A Greek Countryside. The Southern Argolid from Prehistory to the Present Day*, Stanford.

Jones, A., 2007. *Memory and Material Culture*, Cambridge.

Khazanov, A.M., 1983. *Nomads and the Outside World*, Cambridge.

Khazanov, A.M., 1998. 'Pastoralists in the Contemporary World: The Problem of Survival', *Changing Nomads in a Changing World*, J. Ginat and A. M. Khazanov (eds.), Brighton, 7-23.

Korres, G., 1978. 'Βοϊδοκοιλιά' *Εργον*, 46-7.

Korres, G., 1990. 'Excavations in the Region of Pylos', *Eymousia. Ceramic and Iconographic Studies in honour of Alexander Cambitoglou*, J.-P. Descœudres (ed.), Sydney, 1-11.

Korres, G., 1993. 'Messenia and its Commercial Connections in the Bronze Age', *Proceedings of the International Conference Wace and Blegen. Pottery as Evidence for trade in the Aegean Bronze Age 1939-1989*, C. Zerner, P. Zerner and J. Winder (eds.), Amsterdam, 231-48.

Kristiansen, K., 2005. 'What Language did Neolithic Pots Speak? Colin Renfrew's European Farming-Language-Dispersal Model Challenged', *Antiquity* 79, 679-91.

Kyrieleis, H., 1990. 'Neue Ausgrabungen in Olympia', *Antike Welt* 21, 177-88.

Kyrieleis, H., 2006. *Anfänge und Frühzeit des Heiligtums von Olympia. Die Ausgrabungen am Pelopion 1987-1996.* Berlin.

Lewis, N.N., 1987. *Nomads and Settlers in Syria and Jordan 1800-1980.* Cambridge.

Lillios, K.T., 1999. 'Objects of Memory: The Ethnography and Archaeology of Heirlooms', *Journal of Archaeological Method and Theory* 6, 235-62.

Lancaster, W. and Lancaster, F., 1998. 'Who are these Nomads? What do they do? Continuous Change or Changing Continuities', *Changing Nomads in a Changing World*, J. Ginat and A. M. Khazanov (eds.), Brighton, 24-37.

Manning, S., 1997. 'Cultural Change in the Aegean c. 2200 BC', *Third Millennium BC Climate Change and Old World Collapse*, H. Nüzhet Dalfes, G. Kukla and H. Weiss (eds.), Berlin, 149-71.

Maran, J., 1986. 'Überlegungen zur Abkunft der FH III-zeitlichen ritz- und einstichverzierten Keramik', *Hydra* 2, 1-28.

Maran, J., 1998. *Kulturwandel auf dem griechischen Festland und den Kykladen im späten 3. Jahrtausend v. Chr. Studien zu den kulturellen Verhältnissen in Südosteuropa und dem zentralen sowie östlichen Mittelmeerraum in der späten Kupfer- und frühen Bronzezeit.* Bonn.

Maran, J., 2007. 'Seaborne Contacts between the Aegean, the Balkans and the Central Mediterranean in the 3rd Millennium BC: The Unfolding of the Mediterranean World',

Between the Aegean and Baltic Seas. *Prehistory across Borders*, I. Galanaki, H. Tomas, Y. Galanakis and R. Laffineur (eds.), [Aegaeum 27], Liège, 3-21.

Mee, C., 2001. 'Nucleation and Dispersal in Neolithic and Early Helladic Laconia', *Urbanism in the Aegean Bronze Age*, K. Branigan (ed.), Sheffield, 1-14.

Moreland, J., 2001. *Archaeology and Text*, London.

Müller, S., 1989. 'Les tumuli helladiques: où? quand? comment?', *Bulletin de Correspondance Hellénique* 113, 1-42.

Okely, J., 1983. *The Traveller-Gypsies*, Cambridge.

Pullen, D.J., 1992. 'Ox and Plow in the Early Bronze Age Aegean', *American Journal of Archaeology* 96, 45-54.

Rambach, J., 2002. 'Olympia. 2500 Jahre Vorgeschichte vor der Gründung des eisenzeitlichen Heiligtums', *Olympia 1875-2000. 125 Jahre Deutsche Ausgrabungen*, H. Kyrieleis (ed.), Berlin, 177-212.

Renfrew, C., 2004. 'Towards a Theory of Material Engagement', *Rethinking Materiality. The Engagement of Mind with the Material World*, E. DeMarrais, C. Gosden and C. Renfrew (eds.), Cambridge, 23-31.

Rosen, A.M., 1997. 'Environmental Change and Human Adaptational Failure at the End of the Early Bronze Age in the Southern Levant', *Third Millennium BC Climate Change and Old World Collapse*, H. Nüzhet Dalfes, G. Kukla and H. Weiss (eds.), Berlin, 25-38.

Rutter, J., 1982. 'A Group of Distinctive Pattern-Decorated Early Helladic III Pottery from Lerna and its Implications', *Hesperia* 51, 459-488.

Rutter, J., 1988. 'Early Helladic III Vasepainting, Ceramic Regionalism and the Influence of Basketry', *Problems in Greek Prehistory*, E. French and K.A. Wardle (eds.), Bristol, 73-89.

Rutter, J., 1990. 'Pottery Groups from Tsoungiza at the End of the Middle Bronze Age', *Hesperia* 57, 375-458.

Rutter, J., 1995. *Lerna Volume III. The Pottery of Lerna IV*, Princeton.

Rutter, J., 2001. 'The Prepalatial Bronze Age of the Southern and Central Greek Mainland', *Aegean Prehistory. A Review*, Tracy Cullen (ed.), Boston 95-155.

Sherratt, A., 1981. 'Plough and Pastoralism: Aspects of the Secondary Products Revolution', *Pattern of the Past. Studies in Honour of David Clarke*, I. Hodder, G. Isaac and N. Hammond (eds.), Cambridge, 261-305.

Smith, A.B., 2005. *African Herders. The Emergence of Pastoral Traditions*, Walnut Creek.

Spyropoulos, T., 1981. *Αμφείον. Έραυνα και μελέτη του μνημείου του Αμφείου Θηβών*, Athens.

van Andel, T. and Runnels, C., 1987. *Beyond the Acropolis. A Rural Greek Past*. Stanford.

Weiberg, E. 2007. *Thinking the Bronze Age. Life and Death in Early Helladic Greece*, Uppsala.

Whitelaw, T., 2000. 'Settlement Instability and Landscape Degradation in the Southern Aegean in the Third Millennium', *Landscape and Land Use in Postglacial Greece*, P. Halstead and C. Fredrick (eds.): Sheffield, 135-61.

Whittaker, H., (forthcoming). 'Some Thoughts on Middle Helladic Religious Beliefs and Ritual and their Significance in Relation to Social Structure', *Mesohelladika*, A. Touchais and G. Touchais (eds.), [Bulletin de correspondance hellénique, Supplément].

Wiencke, M.H., 1989. 'Change in Early Helladic II', *American Journal of Archaeology* 93, 495-509.

Williams, H., 2006. *Death and Memory in Early Medieval Britain*, Cambridge.

Zerner, C., 1993. 'New Perspectives on Trade in the Middle and Early Late Helladic Periods on the Mainland', *Proceedings of the International Conference Wace and Blegen. Pottery as Evidence for Trade in the Aegean Bronze Age 1939-1989*, C. Zerner, P. Zerner and J. Winder (eds.), Amsterdam, 39-56.

Zvelebil, M., 1996. 'Farmers our Ancestors and the Identity of Europe', *Cultural Identity and Archaeology. The Construction of European Communities*, P. Graves-Brown, S. Jones and C. Gamble (eds.), London, 145-66.

Old Bulls, New Tricks: The Reinvention of a Minoan Tradition

Kathryn Soar

Introduction

Bull-leaping is the quintessential Minoan performance activity, as it is almost exclusively a Minoan phenomenon. The so-called 'Toreador Fresco' from the Palace of Knossos is one of the most widely known images from the Minoan repertoire, and the subject itself has been discussed and debated since it first become part of the consciousness of Aegean prehistorians. Various viewpoints and perspectives have been offered on the phenomenon of bull-leaping, but as yet no single argument has been firmly accepted as to its function, or indeed whether or not it ever really occurred. Unlike dance and procession, two widely occurring performance activities, bull-leaping still remains an enigma. The majority of discussions on the subject of bull-leaping over the past few decades have mainly focused on reconstruction of its performance (Younger 1995) and of its participants (Damiani-Indelicato 1988) or its setting (Graham 1957; Thompson 1986). More recently, discussions of its function have emerged, with the general consensus that it represents a form of ritual, most likely a rite of passage (Koehl 1986; Saflund 1987; Marinatos 1989; 1993). This paper takes as its starting point the assumption that bull-leaping existed in Minoan Crete as a form of ritual performance.

One intriguing aspect that has mainly been overlooked so far is the wide chronological gap in the depiction of bull-leaping in art, whether in two- or three-dimensional media. Bull-leaping is first represented as far back as the Prepalatial period, where rhyta in the shape of bulls were found at the tholos tombs of Koumasa and Porti, dating to Early Minoan (EM) II (c.2700-2150 BC). The figurine from Koumasa depicts a bull with two small human figures hanging off the bull's horns. Between the horns of the bull (which is exaggeratedly large) is the figure of a leaping acrobat. After this, there is nothing until the Neopalatial period - it is not until Middle Minoan (MM) IIIB/Late Minoan (LM) IA (c.1700-1500 BC) that we find bull-leaping again depicted in the form of a *chryselephantine* figurine of a bull leaper, from the Temple Treasury at Knossos. From then on, bull-leaping becomes one of the most widespread activities depicted in Minoan art in the Neopalatial and Final Palatial periods. So why is there a gap of three hundred years between depictions? Other performance activities, such as dance, appear in performance contexts continuously from the Prepalatial onwards. While we would expect not to find any depictions in wall-painting, that being a phenomena of the New Palace period, bull-leaping is not depicted in either plastic or glyptic media during the Protopalatial period. So why the re-emergence of bull-leaping imagery in the Neopalatial - what were the social and political motivations behind its resurrection?

Bull-Leaping – a brief discussion

The majority of Neopalatial representations of bull-leaping come from the Palace of

Knossos. These include the famous Toreador Fresco from the Court of the Stone Spout, as well as other frescoes from the Northwest Treasure House, the Queen's Megaron and the 'Deposit of High Reliefs'. Other examples from Knossos include a crystal plaque painted with scenes of bull-leaping, as well as a three-dimensional relief wall-painting of a leaper. Although depictions are found outside Knossos, it has been suggested that these originated from the Palace itself (Hallager 1995, 548), and that the rings from Ayia Triada, Zakro and Sklavokambos amongst others were originally produced in a Knossian workshop (Hallager 1995, 549). This has led to the idea that bull-leaping was a purely Knossian event, its use restricted to the Palace or Palatial grounds.

Although no actual evidence survives that definitely places bull-leaping within a palatial setting, it is more than likely that this is where it occurred. The dimensions of the Central Courts of the Minoan palaces have led some scholars to believe they were built with a specific purpose in mind. The proportions of the Central Court (2:1) are repeated in the Central Courts of all the palaces. This uniformity in size and shape may suggest they were constructed to definite specifications for a specific purpose - Graham (1957, 255) likens this to a football field or tennis court. Graham then goes on to discuss the possibility of the Central Court as the venue for the Minoan bull games, as exemplified on the famous Toreador Fresco from the palace of Knossos.

Although artistic representations of bull leaping are not specific as its location, there are hints that it occurs in an urban setting. The Ivory Deposit, found in the 13th magazine in the west wing of the palace of Knossos, consisted of two fragments of wall-painting, one of which preserved the horn and ear of a bull, the other a colonnaded facade, which may be intercepted by the body of a bull (Shaw 1996, 182). Although no remains of leapers have been found in this deposit, the juxtaposition of bull and

architectural element is intriguing. The plaster fragments from another deposit in the 13th magazine include architectural elements, a bull's head and a crowd of male spectators. Cameron reconstructed the fragments into a miniature frieze which depicted a tripartite shrine framed by bull-leapers on one side and spectators on the other (Shaw 1996, 184).

An agate flattened cylinder seal from Priene shows what was originally interpreted as a bull drinking from a trough while a leaper dives down onto its back. Ward (1968, 118) doubts the veracity of the claim that the animal is drinking from a cistern, citing it unlikely that bull would be in a sufficiently placid state to drink while the leaping is taking place. Also, no Minoan cistern similar to this has been found. The pattern, however, suggests a parallel. The block is decorated with diamond shapes, whose only parallels have been found on the niches of a block on the north side of the central court at Phaistos (Thompson 1986, 8).

Further suppositional evidence comes from a related fresco found at the Egyptian site of Tel el Dab'a, on the Eastern Delta, the ancient site of Avaris. This particular fresco has been named the 'Bull and Maze' fresco, and shows a bull-leaping scene against a maze-like pattern backdrop. This is the only site outside the Aegean where such bull-leaping frescoes are found (although it is also depicted on Syrian cylinder seals from around 1700 BC), and it is possible that it is from Knossos itself that the inspiration may have come (Shaw 1995, 93). The action in the fresco clearly takes place on paved ground, and it has been proposed that the maze is artistic shorthand for palatial grounds, with the maze pattern replicating the design of a Minoan floor (Bietak et al. 2000, 81). Parallels between the maze pattern in art and the idea of the Palace of Knossos as a 'labyrinth' are also intriguing.

All this evidence may be circumstantial, but in lieu of any firm evidence for the location of bull leaping activities, the setting of the Central Court is certainly a valid hypothesis.

If the Neopalatial evidence is compared to that of the Prepalatial, the location of its occurrence is striking. The Prepalatial evidence comes from the tholos tombs of the Mesara region in south-central Crete. These tombs represent the community - they are the basis of regional ritual during the Prepalatial period and emphasise a group or community irrespective of whether such an egalitarian ideology actually existed in reality (Soar forthcoming). We do not know for definite where bull-leaping took place during the Prepalatial. It is doubtful that such an event would take place at the tholoi, in the paved areas in the front, due to their small size. But the discovery of several representations of bull leaping in the tholoi suggests some kind of connection between these communal burial areas and the act of bull leaping.

Ideologically, the use of the Central Courts as the location for Minoan sports is worlds apart from the tholos tombs of the Prepalatial period, with their emphasis on communality.

These locations are places for human interaction, culturally defined settings for diverse public interactions. The form of interaction depends on what can be reconstructed and inferred from the messages that these spaces still transmit.

The paved areas of the tholos tombs represent a performance space with very little division, if any, between spectator and performer. For a start, the relative distance between the tholos tombs which have enclosed areas and settlement sites is minimal. The furthest distance is located at Lebena, and there the distance between tomb and settlement is less than 400m (Branigan 1997, 17). At the other sites, the distance varies between 50m and 250m. This suggests that these tombs were very much an integral part of the settlement and incorporated into its worldview. The relative size of the paved or enclosed area also suggests that it could

incorporate the majority of the settlement population within it. At Koumasa, for example, the paving extended over 50m by 8m, bounded by a straight wall (Branigan 1997, 21). The enclosed area at Ayia Kyriaki, which although not paved showed evidence of trampled ground within a space enclosed by a peribolos wall, measured approximately 5m across at its widest and 9m at its longest. It has been argued that the tomb at Ayia Kyriaki was used by three nuclear families each with an approximate size of five to six persons, for a period of 800 to 900 years (Murphy 1997, 31). Although it is notoriously difficult to deduce prehistoric population densities, and this estimate is for but one of the several tholos tombs discussed here, nonetheless if this is a correct, the paved and enclosed spaces were more than sufficient to hold this number of people. This suggests that the paved or enclosed areas of the cemetery sites were intended for the community as a whole, acting as the focus of communal life (Branigan 1970, 138). This communal aspect may also be shown by the location of the paved or enclosed areas. For example, at Platanos the location of the paved area between tombs A and B suggests it may have been a common area belonging to all the tombs, rather than for one specific tomb (Murphy 2003, 228).

Internally, the paved or enclosed areas are relatively spacious, in the sense that there is little architectural material inside them - they are simply open spaces, enclosed by a wall. There is no division within the space - no causeways or internal walls. The enclosed spaces are not overlooked by any platforms or grandstands, and are in most cases located on relatively flat land, visible to anyone approaching the tomb or viewing it from the nearby settlement. Any person or people performing on these enclosed spaces would have been visible not only to those also performing, but to anyone viewing the performance from the settlement.

The Central Court, it has been argued, was a semi-public space, an area that was used for public use that was 'under conditions' and restricted (Palyvou 2004, 209). This semi-public status can be demonstrated by the restricted and controlled access, which developed with the construction of the new palaces in early LM IA, in comparison with the more accessible Middle Minoan buildings. The outer, west courts of the palaces have raised walkways, which cross the open space of the West Court and then some of them, such as the causeway at the south Entrance of the Palace of Knossos (which continues into and along the Corridor of Procession), lead into the palace, stopping when they reach the Central Court. Driessen (2004, 79) describes the raised causeways as effecting a transition from a publicly-viewed world into another, hermetically sealed off. Its lack of visibility from outside – nobody standing outside the Palace would be able to see the Central Court. This introverted aspect of the Central Court is emphasised by the fact the Central Court has no focal point in itself, but is itself the focal point of the Palace, which looks at the inside, rather than the outside (Panagiotopoulos 2006, 32). Overall then, the 'message' of the Central Court is one of exclusion, despite its large size. Although the architectural setting does not directly inform us as to the form of performance which may have occurred, these spaces do inform us as to the perspectives involved within this performance and, by default, hint at the ideologies which produced them.

But what does this suggest about the *function* of bull-leaping in the Neopalatial period? To understand this it is necessary to contextualise this kind of performance against the political backdrop of the Neopalatial period.

Crete in the Neopalatial Period

Recent debates on political structure during the Neopalatial period of Crete have rejected the previously held belief of a hierarchical centralised polity based at Knossos. Material homogeneity in architectural forms, pottery styles and administrative practices, amongst others, has been interpreted as an indication of a large, island-wide integrating political structure with dependent centres emulating the main political centre, i.e. Knossos (Schoep 2002, 22). The similarities in function and style between the various palaces of the Neopalatial period have also been interpreted as less grandiose repetitions by lower order centres of the functions exerted by the capital. Again, this can be considered an argument in favour of a single integrated political organisation with a single centre (Schoep 2002, 22). A continuation of this line of thought is the interpretation of the proliferation of palatial architecture in the country-houses at the beginning of the LM IA as the formation of an extra hierarchical level: that of secondary elite, subordinate to the palatial elite present at the larger centres. The site hierarchies can further support the idea that Knossos, as the largest site, was indeed the political centre of the island (Vansteenhuyse 2002, 243).

However, recent analysis has called the veracity of the Knossos-centric idea into question. A new examination of the state of the Late Bronze Age political landscape has suggested alternatives to this theory, and the stated reasons that suggest a Knossos-centric model have been challenged.

Most importantly new interpretations have stressed that instead of cultural homogeneity, regional dynamics were instead manifest across the landscape (Schoep 2002, 23). The idea of a contemporary horizon for the construction of palaces and villas in MM IIIB and early LM IA may in fact be an illusion, as recent work suggests that the Palace at Phaistos was not built until LM IB and Zakro palace not built until late LM IA (Schoep 2002, 23). The size and monumentality of Knossos may also not be as important as has been previously stressed, as excavations report that Knossos was larger than other sites even as far back as the Neolithic, so size itself cannot be taken to indicate political authority (Hamilakis 2002, 183). An analysis of material culture - pottery, architecture and administrative evidence, such as tablets - also suggests that it was not as homogenous as previously assumed. Although the evidence integrates some island-wide styles and fashions, it also displays regional characteristics (Schoep 2002, 23). The so-called villas also appear to have had settlements surrounding them, rather than being isolated country houses, suggesting they many have been centres of authority and power in their own right (Hamilakis 2002, 183). Further to this, homogeneity of material culture does not necessarily automatically equate with imposition of style; other processes such as emulation and competition might be involved (Hamilakis 2002, 183).

These arguments have stressed the idea that political structures in the Neopalatial period were not as rigid as previously considered, but instead were more unstable and fluid than was thought (see Adams 2004). This has led to the idea of Neopalatial Crete representing a heterarchical political structure. Heterarchy may be defined as the relation of elements to one another when they are unranked or when they possess the potential for being ranked in a number of different ways (Crumley 1995, 3). With heterarchy, forms of order exist that are not exclusively hierarchical, and interactive elements in complex systems need not be permanently ranked relative to one another (Crumley 1995, 3). The notion of heterarchy allows us to rank social elements in a multiplicity of ways depending on their contexts, freeing us to consider life at the community level and to view the regional system from the bottom-up rather than simply as unilineal hierarchy from the top-down (Mehrer 2000, 46). Heterarchy emphasises the decentralised nature of power (Parkinson and Galaty 2007, 116). As noted earlier, heterarchical does not necessarily equate to egalitarian, and so there is still evidence for elite levels within a heterarchical society -heterarchy and hierarchy can work for each other, as well as against each other, within a single system (Schoep and Knappett 2005, 23). A heterarchical society can include levels of inequality and dominance; they are not promoted by a single central authority, but rather by a diversity of groups (Brumfiel 1995, 129). One aspect of this is factional competition.

Factions and Factional Competition

Factions are one potential method for archaeologists to conceptualise power relations in a way that is not purely hierarchical, although elements of hierarchy often come into play. Factions are generally groups in which leaders hold similar social positions, are organised in and function in similar ways, and they compete with one another for resources and positions of power (Conlee 2005, 212). Factions compete for material and social resources and mainly for the attraction, recruitment and retention of retinue, in order to gain social power (Hamilakis 1998, 233). They are united by cosmologies and ideologies, and these competitions can take the form of material culture 'wars'.

Evidence from the Neopalatial period on Crete could indicate that social and political organisation was of competing factions. The palaces and villas may have operated as the base of factions of different size, and socio-political influence (Hamilakis 2002, 188). In this sense, palaces are only one aspect of a wider process, and may represent the base of the most successful faction at the time, rather than being ends by themselves (Hamilakis 1988, 234).

Evidence from these palaces suggests that there was an unusually intensive level of hierarchical socio-political competition at Neopalatial Knossos, attested by the trappings of power. These include building materials, decoration and administrative power, which were displayed in an elaborate and monumental manner. The use of ashlar and gypsum, for example, is only used selectively in Neopalatial towns, and predominately at Knossos, where it may have acted as an elite symbol within construction to underline group membership (Driessen 1999, 229). Analysis of the buildings in the town of Knossos suggests intense formalisation of ceremonial activities, which may be an emulation of the Palace's architecture. It has been suggested that this represents competition between those responsible for commissioning the buildings (Adams 2004, 210). There is also evidence for idiosyncratic ritual buildings in the towns, again suggesting that elite architectural assemblage was restricted to certain buildings, which would have excluded certain members of the community (Adams 2004, 210). The town at Knossos appears to be tiered, in terms of buildings at least, with the Palace at the top, followed by grand mansions, specialised buildings and finally less elaborate houses (Adams 2004, 212). Similar examples of this tiering system appear in other towns, such as Malia. The presence of a tiered social system may have led to factional competition between the premier elites (those of the Palace), and the second-tiers and below. This palatial elite may have displayed the trappings of their power via monumental and elaborate features in order to reaffirm their status for fear of losing it (Adams 2004, 213). The evidence from various towns also suggests that factions and factional competition may have operated primarily at local and regional levels, where immediate social interaction would have been easier (Hamilakis 2002, 188).

One area that is an especially common arena for political competition is the feast. Hamilakis (1998; 1999; 2002) has studied the use of feasting and conspicuous consumption as an element of factional competition within Neopalatial society. He has argued that an analysis of food remains and pottery, as well as other artefacts associated with food consumption reveal intensive episodes of feasting at centre centres, such as palaces and palatial villas (Hamilakis 1998, 234). During the Neopalatial, the most evidence for wine production was found, as well as the production of masses of drinking and serving vessels. Taken together with the 'explosion' in elaboration of material culture of this period, this suggests complex social interactions characterised by intense competition for retinue and resources, of which feasting was an important element in the elites competition for authority and control (Hamilakis 1999, 48).

Evidence of performance in the Neopalatial period fits in with the idea of competition which is inherent within feasting and factionalism. Representations of performance in this period include an element of competitiveness and display which does not appear to occur in earlier periods. This is most obvious in the scenes of competitive sports - boxing, wrestling, bull-leaping. But depictions of activities such as dancing, which had appeared in the Minoan artistic repertoire since the Prepalatial, appear to have a new element of display in the Neopalatial, exemplified most famously by the Sacred Grove and Dance fresco wherein a select group of presumably elite females dance before a large audience.

The idea of bodily senses being utilised within factional competition is important in examining the role that performance may have taken within this sphere. Ethnographic studies have pointed to the importance of performance, more specifically elite performance, within the sphere of political behaviour and patronage (e.g. Beekman 2000). Like feasting, performances take place before and are witnessed by followers, with the aim of gathering followers among commoners, and building alliances to gain adherents among other elites. That followers witnessed or even participated in these occasions was vitally important, as they were not just simply entertainment, but an opportunity for factions to display their power and connections in a bid for the kind of wealth that would matter the most in a pre-industrial society - people (Beekman 2000, 388). Public performances would not only emphasise particular factions and gather adherents through this mechanism, but the labour pool to which the faction would now have access could allow even more ostentatious ceremony at future events (Beekman 2000, 393).

However, performances cannot simply be viewed as tools of ideological propaganda, but instead they may have acted as arenas of negotiation and conflict of power. The strong emphasis on *public* performance by the factions may imply they were under constant check by their peers and subjects (Inomata 2006, 211). These events may have been critical arenas where communities were reconstituted and asymmetrical power relations were imposed, negotiated and resisted (Inomata 2006, 213).

Use of the term 'competition' while discussing factionalism in Neopalatial Crete suggests that there would be a 'winner' amongst the competing factions. It has been suggested that perhaps the palaces were seats of these factions, with Knossos, as the largest of these, being the seat of the prevailing group (Hamilakis 2002, 188; Parkinson and Galaty 2007, 120). It is entirely possible that the same group remained in power throughout the entirety of the Neopalatial period, as there is no evidence to suggest a regular or even occasional disruption in function or utilisation of the Palace, aside from the obvious destruction levels which characterise the end of the Protopalatial and Neopalatial periods. However, awareness of the existence of competitive factions within the Knossos area, and within Crete as a whole, may have stimulated the Knossian faction, leading them to constantly reaffirm their position within society via the medium of ostentatious feasting and display.

If this is true, and Knossos was the seat of the dominant faction, then it is interesting that depictions of bull leaping only occur at that site.

Memory, Tradition and Identity

Bull leaping at Knossos may well represent an ideological tool for the 'ruling' faction, a form of ritual performance that only they were permitted access to. By the Neopalatial period, some thousand years had passed since the introduction of bull-leaping in the Prepalatial. By re-introducing it into the socio-political arena of the Neopalatial, the ruling faction could have been emphasising their hereditary claim, calling up distant cultural memories for their own political gain. It is noteworthy that this performance may have occurred on the Central Courts of the Palace. Aside from the ideological message which was conveyed by these specific spaces, they also represent a continuous link with the past. Beneath the Central Court at Knossos were remains from the Aceramic Neolithic period, consisting of a small amount of chipped stone tools and four obsidian artefacts (Efstratiou *et al* 2004, 45) in a stratum 10-30cm thick (Perlès 2001, 68). These represent the earliest remains on the island (Panagiotopoulos 2006, 34). The occupation of Knossos continues through the Early Neolithic, being the only settlement site known from this period, the other evidence coming from cave sites (Tomkins and Day 2001, 259). The foundations upon which the Central Court was built represent the longest continual link with the past anywhere on the island. The builders of Knossos may have used this space to instrumentalise the existence of the earliest settlement and form a link with it by placing the Central Court of the ruling faction on this spot (Panagiotopoulos 2006, 34).

Associated with this idea of connection to the past is that of bull-leaping representing an invented tradition. Invented traditions are a set of practices which seek to inculcate certain values and norms by repetition by creating a link with the past. These practices are governed by accepted rules, and are of ritual or symbolic nature (Hobsbawm 1983, 1) In the course of this, bodily practice and performance are manipulated and utilised to imply continuity with the past, whether or not this is largely fictitious. We have already noted the possible use of the Central Court as a performance space to instrumentalise a link to the past. The use of a performance act at this particular site which had occurred in the past but had subsequently disappeared further accentuated the connection between the ruling faction and the past.

Bull-leaping in the Neopalatial, however, is not an exact replica of bull-leaping as it was (presumably) performed in the Prepalatial. As a practice it had previously been linked to ideas of community and egalitarianism, but was now strictly regulated, regimented and accessible only to a few. It was a tradition which had been reinvented and adapted. Shils (1971, 133) argues that the need to be connected with the past is often more intense amongst those who seek to 'create a past' for themselves, in order to legitimate themselves in a way for which just 'being themselves' in the present does not permit. The search for past practices and beliefs to replace current ones sometimes discovers beliefs that were once accepted or widespread within the seeker's own society; the recreated tradition need not necessarily have ever have existed in the form in which the seeker alleges, the emphasis lies in the seeker's belief that it did (Shils 1971, 133). Such a scenario may well have occurred with the act of bull-leaping in the Neopalatial period, with its roots as a communal performative act in the Prepalatial reinterpreted as an elite event in the later period. The 'creation of a past' would have been a useful tool for the ruling faction at Knossos to legitimate their ascendant position. Because traditional rituals have conservative properties, they are an ideal way for emerging rulers to insert and justify their own political agendas (Lucero 2003, 525). New political systems borrow legitimacy from the old by nurturing the old ritual forms, redirected to new purposes (Kertzer 1988, 42). In more recent history, the appropriation of cultural practices of the rural peasantry or of the urban lower classes by the state has been a persistent strategy in

the development of national cultures throughout the world, whether as indications of the dominance of one specific group or as displays of cultural pluralism (Reed 1998, 511). The familiarity of strategic rituals is what causes them to be successful and to situate the growing political power of a specific corporate group; abrupt change would be much more likely to fail, being viewed as foreign or unacceptable (Lucero 2003, 525). Aspects of tradition are often appropriated either in whole or in part, and the connections between the past, present and future are framed as a manifestation of destiny (Cobb and King 2005, 172).

The re-introduction of past ritual would enable the ruling faction to develop their own specific identity, to distinguish them from other factions within Neopalatial society who may not have been as successful. Creating or reinventing history is a way of producing identity, as it produces a relation between that which supposedly occurred in the past and the present socio-political situation (Friedman 1992, 837). Political leaders will often adopt an identity that has historical weight and meaning (Stockett 2007, 92). However, this identity has to be mediated through action and the repetition of practice, a form of which is ritual, which can have the power to generate responses of affiliation underlying specific identities (Stockett 2007, 92). Thus the utilisation of the past in the present is a dynamic force, one which needs constant repetition to remain effective. The frequency of bull-leaping imagery from the Neopalatial onwards, especially in comparison to other forms of performance activities, would suggest that bull-leaping was a performance which occurred, if not regularly, then on more than one occasion.

As we have seen, the reuse of the past is an 'incorporated' practice, based on embodied enactments and re-enactments of physical acts, a sensory experience that will transmit a memory of other such acts which have been performed before, as well as creating a memory for the present (Weiberg 2007, 105).

This allows people distanced temporally from the original performance to retain and repeat it, as well as intentionally or unconsciously restructure, transform, or accentuate some of the intentions and results of that act, in order to generate new memories (Weiberg 2007, 105). These developments suggest official changes were introduced to bring rituals into line with new social realities, and a specialised kind of communication during which the past is re-enacted in the present.

Other evidence from Knossos also suggests that a link to the past was an important feature in the Neopalatial. One example of this comes from a store of Neolithic pottery found with LM I sherds in an artificial cave in the Pillar Crypt of the Southeast House at Knossos. The sealing of these representations of the past within a ritual context may suggest a deliberate binding of the distant past with the present (Adams 2007, 413). In this case, the link with the past is empirical and material. With bull-leaping, the link to the past was engaged via ritual and performance, through bodily memory and enacted tradition.

In the case of bull-leaping, the leading Neopalatial faction at Knossos took a past tradition and wove it into the present in order to assure their future. By immortalising this practice in various forms of artwork, they also made it timeless.

References

Adams, E., 2004. 'Power Relations in Minoan Palatial Towns: An Analysis of Neopalatial Knossos and Malia', *Journal of Mediterranean Archaeology* 17.2, 191-222

Adams, E., 2007. 'Time and Chance: Unravelling Temporality in North-Central Neopalatial Crete', *American Journal of Archaeology* 111, 391-421

Alcock, S.E., 2002. *Archaeologies of the Greek Past: Landscape, Monuments and Memories.* Cambridge.

Beekman, C.S. 2000. 'The Correspondence of Regional Patterns and Local Strategies in Formative to Classic Period West Mexico', *Journal of Anthropological Archaeology* 19.4, 385-412

Bietak, M., Marinatos, N. and Palyvou, C., 2000. 'The Maze Tableau from Tell el Dab'a', *The Wall Paintings of Thera*, S. Sherratt (ed.), Athens, 77-90.

Branigan, K., 1970. *The Tombs of Mesara. A Study of Funerary Architecture and Ritual in Southern Crete, 2800-1700 B.C.*, London.

Branigan, K., 1997. 'The Nearness of You: Proximity and Distance in Early Minoan Funerary Behaviour', *Cemetery and Society in the Aegean Bronze Age*, K. Branigan (ed.), [Sheffield Studies in Aegean Archaeology 1], Sheffield, 13-26.

Brumfiel, E., 2005. 'Heterarchy and the Analysis of Complex Societies', *Heterarchy and the Analysis of Complex Societies*, R. Ehrenreich, C. Crumley, and E. Brumfiel (eds.), [Archeological Papers of the American Anthropological Association 6], Washington DC, 125–31.

Cobb, C.R. and King, A., 2005. 'Re-Inventing Mississippian Tradition at Etowah,

Georgia', *Journal of Archaeological Method and Theory* 12.3, 167-92

Conlee, C.A., 2005. 'The Expansion, Diversification, and Segmentation of Power in Late Prehispanic Nasca', *The Foundations of Power in the Prehispanic Andes*, K.J. Vaughn, D.E. Ogburn, and C.A. Conlee (eds.), [Archeological Papers of the American Anthropological Association 14], Washington DC, 211-23.

Crumley, C., 1995. 'Heterarchy and the Analysis of Complex Societies: Comments', *Heterarchy and the Analysis of Complex Societies*, R. Ehrenreich, C. Crumley, and E. Brumfiel (eds.) [Archeological Papers of the American Anthropological Association 6.], Washington DC, 1-5.

Damiani-Indelicato, S., 1988. 'Were Cretan Girls Playing at Bull-Leaping?', *Cretan Studies* 1, 39-47

Driessen, J., 1999. 'The Dismantling of a Minoan Hall at Palaikastro (Knossians Go Home?)', *Meletemata: Studies in Aegean Archaeology Presented to Malcolm H. Wiener as He Enters His 65th Year*, P.P. Betancourt, V. Karageorghis, R. Laffineur, and W.-D. Niemeier (eds.), [Aegaeum 20], Liège, 227-36.

Driessen, J., 2004. 'The Central Court of the Palace at Knossos', *Knossos: Palace, City, State*, G. Cadogan, E. Hatzaki and A. Vasilakis (eds.), [British School at Athens Studies 12], London, 75-83.

Efstratiou, N., Karetsou, A., Banou, S. and Margomenou D., 2004. 'The Neolithic Settlement at Knossos: New Light on an Old Picture', *Knossos: Palace, City, State*, G. Cadogan, E. Hatzaki and A. Vasilakis (eds.), [British School at Athens Studies 12], London, 39-49.

Graham, J.W., 1957. 'The Central Court as the Minoan Bull Ring', *American Journal of Archaeology* 61, 255-62

Hallager, B.P. and Hallager, E., 1995. 'The Knossian Bull – Political Propaganda in Neo-Palatial Crete?, *Politeia: Society and State in the Aegean Bronze Age*, R. Laffineur and W.D. Niemeier (eds.), [Aegeaum 12], Liège, 547-56.

Hamilakis, Y., 1998. 'Consumption Patterns, Factional Competition and Political Development in Bronze Age Crete', *Bulletin of the Institute of Classical Studies* 42, 233-34

Hamilakis, Y., 1999. 'Food Technologies/Technologies of the Body: the Social Context of Wine and Oil Production and Consumption in Bronze Age Crete', *World Archaeology* 31.1, 38-54

Hamilakis, Y., 2002. 'Too Many Chiefs?: Factional Competition in Neopalatial Crete', *Monuments of Minos. Rethinking the Minoan Palaces*, J. Driessen, I. Schoep and R. Laffineur (eds.) [Aegeaum 23], Liege, 179-99.

Hobsbawm, E., 1983. 'Introduction: Inventing Traditions', *The Invention of Tradition*, E. Hobsbawm and T. Ranger (eds.), Cambridge, 1-14.

Inomata, T., 2006. 'Politics and Theatricality in Mayan Society', *Archaeology of Performance*: *Theaters of Power, Community, and Politics*, T. Inomata and L. Coben (eds.), Oxford, 187-222.

Kertzer, D.I., 1988. *Ritual, Politics and Power*, New Haven.

Koehl, R.B., 1986. 'The Chieftain Cup and a Minoan Rite of Passage', *Journal of Hellenic Studies* 106, 99-110.

Lucero, L.J., 2003. 'The Politics of Ritual: The Emergence of Classic Maya Rulers', *Current Anthropology* 44.4, 523-58.

Marinatos, N., 1993. *Minoan Religion: Ritual, Image and Symbol*, Columbia.

Mehrer, M.W., 2000. 'Heterarchy and Hierarchy: The Community Plan as Institution at Cahokia's Polity', *The Archaeology of Communities*, M.A. Canuto and J. Yaeger (eds.), London, 44-57.

Murphy, J.M., 1997. 'Ideologies, Rites and Rituals: A View of Prepalatial Minoan Tholoi', *Cemetery and Society in the Aegean Bronze Age*, K. Branigan (ed.), [Sheffield Studies in Aegean Archaeology 1], Sheffield, 27-40.

Murphy, J.M., 2003. *Changing Roles and Locations of Religious Practices in South Central Crete during the Pre-Palatial and Proto-Palatial Periods*. Unpublished PhD dissertation, University of Cincinnati.

Palyvou, C., 2004. 'Outdoor Space in Minoan Architecture: "Community and Privacy,"', *Knossos: Palace, City, State*, G. Cadogan, E. Hatzaki and A. Vasilakis (eds.) [British School at Athens Studies 12], London, 207-17.

Panagiotopoulos, D., 2006. 'Der Minoische 'Hof' als Kulisse zeremonieller Handlug', *Constructing Power: Architecture, Ideology and Social Practice*, J. Maran, C.J.H. Schwengel and U. Thaler (eds.), [Geschichter Forschung und Wissenschaft: 19], Hamburg, 31-48.

Parkinson, W.A. and Galaty, M., 2007. 'Secondary States in Perspective: An Integrated Approach to State Formation in the Prehistoric Aegean', *American Anthropologist* 109.1, 113-29.

Perlès, C., 2001. *The Early Neolithic in Greece. The First Farming Communities in Europe*, Cambridge.

Reed, S.A. 1998. 'The Politics and Poetics of Dance', *Annual Review of Anthropology* 27, 503-32.

Saflund, G., 1987. 'The Agoge of the Minoan Youth as Reflected by Palatial Iconography', *The Function of the Minoan Palaces*, R. Hägg and N. Marinatos (eds.), [Skrifter Utgivna av Svenska Institut I Athen, 35], Stockholm, 227-33.

Schoep, I., 2002. 'The State of the Minoan Palaces or the Minoan Palace-State?', *Monuments of Minos. Rethinking the Minoan Palaces*, J. Driessen, I. Schoep and R. Laffineur (eds.), [Aegaeum 23], Liège, 15-33.

Schoep, I. and Knappett, C., 2005. 'Dual Emergence: Evolving Heterarchy, Exploding Hierarchy', *The Emergence of Civilisation Revisited*, J. Barrett and P. Halstead (eds.) [Sheffield Studies in Aegean Archaeology 6], Oxford, 21-37.

Shaw, M.C., 1995. 'Bull Leaping Frescoes at Knossos and their Influence on the Tell el-Dab'a Murals', *Trade, Power and Cultural Exchange: Hyksos Egypt and the Eastern Mediterranean World 1800-1500 B.C.*, M. Bietak (ed.), [Ägypten und Levante 5], Wien, 91-120.

Shaw, M.C., 1996. 'The Bull-Leaping Fresco from below the Ramp House at Mycenae: A Study in Iconography and Artistic Transmission', *Annual of the British School at Athens* 91, 167-190.

Shils, E., 1971. 'Traditions', *Comparative Studies in History and Society* 13.2, 122-59.

Soar, K., (forthcoming). 'Dying to be Different: Performance and Social Differentiation in Prepalatial Crete', *SOMA 2007: Symposium on Mediterranean Archaeology*, Ç. Özkan Aygün (ed.), [BAR International Series], Oxford.

Stockett, M., 2007. 'Performing Power: Identity, Ritual, and Materiality in a Late Classic Southeast Mesoamerican Crafting Community', *Ancient Mesoamerica* 18, 91-105.

Thompson, J.G., 1986. 'The Location of the Minoan Bull Sports: A Consideration of the Problem', *Journal of Sport History* 13.1, 5-13.

Tomkins, P. and Day, P.M. 2001. 'Production and Exchange of the Earliest Ceramic Vessels in the Aegean: View from Early Neolithic Knossos, Crete', *Antiquity* 75.228, 259-60.

Vansteenhuyse, K., 2002. 'Minoan Courts and Ritual Competition', *Monuments of Minos. Rethinking the Minoan Palaces*, J. Driessen, I. Schoep and R. Laffineur (eds.), [Aegaeum 23], Liège, 235-48.

Ward, A., 1968. 'The Cretan Bull Sports', *Antiquity* 42.166, 117-122.

Weiberg, E., 2007. *Thinking the Bronze Age. Life and Death in Early Helladic Greece*, [Boreas. Uppsala Studies in Ancient Mediterranean and Near Eastern Civilizations 44], Stockholm.

Younger, J., 1995. 'Bronze Age Representations of Aegean Bull-Leaping, III', *Politeia: Society and State in the Aegean Bronze Age,* R. Laffineur and W.D. Niemeier (eds.), [Aegaeum 12], Liège, 507-45.

The East Aegean-Western Anatolia in the Late Bronze Age III: what do the tombs tell us about memory, tradition and identity?

Mercourios Georgiadis

Introduction

The studies concerning the East Aegean-Western Anatolia for the Late Bronze Age, are haunted by the *Ahhiyawa* problem. The Hittite texts are the prime source evoked, whilst the use of archaeological evidence is limited and often enough superficial. For the scholars whose main concern is Anatolia the main question posed is the geographical position of *Ahhiyawa* and *Millawanda* in Western Anatolia in order to reconstruct the map of Late Bronze Age in this region. For the researchers that are mainly interested in Mycenaean Greece the core of the *Ahhiyawa* issue is the extent and character of the Greek mainland power over the Aegean.

The present analysis will offer both outlooks adding aspects that have not drawn enough attention. It will be attempted to bridge the gap between the Anatolian and the Mycenaean angle of enquiry by centering our attention in the region under question. More importantly a contextual approach taking into account spatial and temporal aspects will be offered. The combination of the textual evidence and the information they offer with the archaeological evidence from the East Aegean-Western Anatolia will allow us to appreciate fully the socio-political processes that were under way during this period. Thus, a deeper understanding of the specific region will be achieved, highlighting its independent role and not just as a buffer zone between the Mycenaeans and the Hittites. The archaeological data that will be used will rely heavily on the burial context since there are more than 60 cemeteries recovered throughout this region in contrast to the very few settlement excavations. These finds are the result of interaction and exchanges between mainland Greece and Western Anatolia. Moreover, the funerary context offers a symbolic space where ideas and meanings can be transmitted, altered and manipulated according to the desires and beliefs of the participants. Hence, new traditions were formed incorporating foreign imports in which a symbolic significance was attributed to them. Through these traditions new aspects on the relation of East Aegean-Western Anatolia with the Greek mainland and Central Anatolia will be highlighted.

The Mycenaean 'expansion'

In order to understand the East Aegean–Western Anatolia it is necessary to place it in the historical and geographical context and with the archaeological evidence available to give a fuller outlook. The critical period is LH IIA-B in mainland Greece and the time the first palaces appeared, with all their socio-political complexity that they symbolize, which they pose an open chronological question (Mylonas 1966, 59; Vermeule 1972, 114; Dickinson 1992, 154, 156; Rutter 1993, 96; Treuil *et al.* 1996, 454-5; Shelmerdine 1997, 558; French 2002, 45-7). I have extensively discussed of the problems the migration and colonization hypotheses pose for this part of the Aegean (Georgiadis 2003; 2004; in press). The important increase of Mycenaean finds and especially the spread of the Greek mainland burial customs in the whole Aegean during LH II-IIIA2 were associated to the Mycenaean expansion to the Aegean.

In the Southeastern Aegean the first chamber tombs appeared in the LH IIB-IIIA1 period at Ialysos and Kos (Furumark 1950, 262-3; Mee 1982, 82; 1988, 301; 1998; Benzi 1992, 212; Taylour 1995, 158, Vasilikou 1995, 388; Karantzali 2001, 78). In the northern part of East Aegean the available data are rather limited and start from the LH IIIA period. Nonetheless there are exceptions as the Mycenaean pottery from Troy testifies, dating from LH IIA onwards (Mee 1978, 147). In this case the pottery recovered comes from the settlement and is of a rather low overall percentage, a situation that lasted until the end of the LH IIIC period. Still, a closer interaction between Troy and mainland Greece existed already established from a rather early date.

The main argument for a Mycenaean rule, which was acquired and retained through military means, has been strongly proposed for Crete (Furumark 1950, 264; Vermeule 1972, 145-6; Kanta 1980, 320; Popham 1980, 166; Watrous 1993, 86; Taylour 1995, 156; Vasilikou 1995, 20-1) and it has been extended to the Cyclades (Barber 1999, 316; Davis and Bennet 1999, 113-4; Deger-Jalkotzy 1999, 124) and eastern Aegean (Macdonald 1985, 192; Mee 1988, 304). At the same time there is the acculturation hypothesis proposed for specific areas such as Crete (Preston 1999, 141-3; 2004, 343) and the South-eastern Aegean (Mountjoy 1998, 51).

Perhaps the answers are more varied than the single explanation offered so far. The close interaction of mainland Greece with the Aegean sites and the successful socio-political structures formed in the mainland was considered desirable by the latter. Hence, a number of elements were adopted intermingled with local practices, traditions and beliefs. This is better demonstrated in the mortuary context and the strong regionalism found in the Aegean sites. This process was multi-faceted and depended upon the local culture, the degree of interaction and interrelation with mainland Greece and the persistence of older traditions. Thus no uniformity should be expected between the Cyclades, Crete and East Aegean-Western Anatolia, even on a regional scale. This proposed model does not exclude small-scale military conflicts between polities, even overseas, the existence of mercenaries and pirates nor small-scale population movement. However these activities should be considered individual events with no long-lasting effects in the local culture such as the enforcement or the adoption of the Mycenaean culture and its socio-political structures.

Mycenaean evidence at East Aegean-Western Anatolia

A large number of cemeteries have been recovered in the Southeastern Aegean islands (Fig.1). The Mycenaean character is seen in the form of the canonical chamber tombs, as well as in the performed rituals and offerings deposited inside at Karpathos, Rhodes, Astypalaia, Kos, Kalymnos, Samos and most probably Ikaria, with local idiosyncrasies and regional characteristics (Georgiadis 2003, 35-43; in press). From unstratified settlement data it seems that Mycenaean pottery evidence occurs at Poli on Kasos (Melas 1985, 83), perhaps at Potamos on Chalki (Melas 1988, 293, 304-7), at the acropolis on Symi (Hope Simpson and Lazenby 1970, 63), at Megalo Chorio on Tilos (Philimonos 1996, 693), close to Mandraki on Nisyros (Melas 1988, 288-92), at the Kastro of Ayia Marina and Partheni on Leros (Hope Simpson and Lazenby 1970, 53-4; Marketou 1980, 557) and at Kastelli on Patmos (Hope Simpson and Lazenby 1970, 48-50).

In the Northeastern Aegean islands there are Mycenaean elements in the construction of tombs and/or in the burial offerings as at Archontiki on Psara (Charitonidis 1961/2b, 256; Achilara 1986, 11; 1996, 1353), Emporio on Chios (Hood 1981, 579-80) and Makara on Lesbos (Charitonidis 1961/2a, 255). Mycenaean material from settlements is found at Kato Phana and Volissos on Chios (Hood 1981, 6, 8), at Thermi, Antissa, Perama and Kourtir on Lesbos (Lamb 1936, 212; Spencer 1995, 275), at Poliochni, Ifestia and Koukonisi on Lemnos (Bernabò-Brea 1976, 336; Boulotis 1997, 267; Messineo 1997, 244-5) and at Imvros (Andreou and Andreou 2001, 145-6; Greaves and Helwing 2001, 502).

In Western Anatolia there are several categories in which we can divide the cemeteries found. At Müskebi (Bass 1963, 353; Hope Simpson 1965, 194; Boysal 1967, 31-4; Mee 1978, 137) and Miletos (Mee 1978, 133-6; Niemeier 1998, 36) we have canonical Mycenaean chamber tombs with the appropriate rituals and offerings placed in them. The same could be applied in the Ayasoluk tomb at Ephesos only that its structure is unclear (Hope Simpson 1965, 193; Boysal 1967, 45-6; Mee 1978, 127). At Kolophon (Bridges 1974, 264-6; Mee 1978, 125-6) the tholos tomb is quite similar to the ones recently found at Kos (Skerlou 1996, 690; 1997), whilst at Bakla Tepe the tomb is of Mycenaean inspiration with a lot of Mycenaean offerings along with the prevailing local ones (Erkanal 1998, 401, 405; IRERP 2000). At Panaztepe oval-shaped and circular tholos tombs were recovered among the cist and pithos burials (Erkanal and Erkanal 1986, 69-72; Ersoy 1988, 59-80; Greaves and Helwing 2003, 94). They appear to be a hybrid between Greek mainland prototypes and local preferences, underlining the degree of Mycenaean influence in this region. Two burial clusters have been found at Troy, one at Beşik Tepe and one 550m from the settlement, where pithos burials predominated (Blegen *et al.* 1953, 370-91;

Korfmann 1986, 21-4; Sperling 1991, 155-6; Mountjoy 1999, 284). Moreover, in the first burial area a built tomb existed, while a number of pottery vessels deposited were Mycenaean, either imported or locally produced. The pots from Kuşadasi (Mee 1978, 132), Pitane (Mee 1978, 143-4) and Çerkes Sultaniye (Hanfmann and Waldbaum 1968, 52) signify the existence of Mycenaean elements in the local burials.

Settlement evidence occurs at several sites in Western Anatolia such as at Cape Krio, Iasos, Mylasa, Stratinikaia, Didyma, Tire-Ahmetler, Erythrai, Smyrna, Larisa, Elaia and Sardis (Mee 1978, 125, 127, 132, 139, 142-4; 1998b, 138; Greaves 2002, 56). More recently Mycenaean material has been recovered at Metropolis few kilometers east of Bakla Tepe (Schachner and Meriç 2000, 99, 101; Greaves and Helwing 2003, 94), as well as at Liman Tepe/Clazomenai close to Smyrna (Greaves and Helwing 2001, 504-6; 2003, 93-4).

Mycenaean material is found in all sites where Late Bronze Age III strata have been recognized (Fig.1). The aforementioned sites total about a hundred, but as yet little evidence has been found in the more inland part of Anatolia. The same applies for the rather limited Hittite items found in the Aegean (Cline 1991a, 1-2; 1991b). Although the excavations in Western Anatolia as well as in the Anatolia hinterland are limited it is clear that there was not much interaction between the Mycenaeans and Central Anatolia. The problem of the material from settlement contexts is that they are mainly unstratified and thus no quantitative or qualitative analysis can be offered about the Mycenaean remains. They only mark direct or indirect interaction, but the extent of the Mycenaean cultural penetration is questionable. According to Mellaart and Murray (1995, 108) Western Anatolia was not influenced by either the Mycenaeans or the Hittites. Hittite finds in Western Anatolia are attested and have influenced to a limited extent the local tradition (Thompson 2007,

96). However, there is no adoption of the Hittite cultural forms and standardization as observed in Cilicia and Central Anatolia up to Gordion (Postgate 2007, 142-4, 149). Thus, a conscious support to the local traditions can be seen, expressing a cultural resistance over the Hittite domination.

There are more than 60 cemeteries in the region under review, in other words almost the two thirds of all the known sites. The mortuary context offers more coherent evidence, better published, and large enough for comparisons. The cemeteries of the islands in the Southeastern Aegean as well the ones at Müskebi and Miletos will be excluded. The reason is that they are canonical Mycenaean not unlike the ones recovered in the Greek mainland, including the rituals and the offerings (Georgiadis 2003). Although this is true, we should not consider them either as one unity or as an implant, since there are several regional differences in this area as well some local characteristics of older traditions. Nonetheless they form a socio-cultural region in contrast to the rest of the cemeteries with Ephesos and Kolophon being at the middle due to the limited archaeological information they provide. In the North-eastern Aegean and North-western Anatolia with the addition of Bakla Tepe there is a far smaller number of cemeteries found, but of considerable differences from the previous group. In this region the earlier tradition of single burials continues to predominate, without the practice of the secondary treatment, while there is frequent use of cremations. In contrast to the South-eastern Aegean the Mycenaean influence in the burial practices is limited to the occasional presence of multiple burials in the form of built tombs and tholoi.

Although this division of north-south is rather oversimplifying and could change with new finds, it could help us to understand the region under study. Hence the northern part of this area will concern us more since the prevailing burial tradition is following the earlier practices. Unlike the southern part, the single burial was favoured in cist, pit and pithos burials, while cremations were frequent at Bakla Tepe and Troy. Nevertheless there are a number of Mycenaean or Mycenaean-inspired elements such as the built tombs at Bakla Tepe, Archontiki, Makara and Beşik Tepe and the tholos tombs at Panaztepe with multiple burials. At the first two sites and specific tombs there is positive evidence of the secondary treatment performed to the deceased (Cavanagh 1978). In all of these cemeteries with the addition of Pitane, Kuşadasi, Çerkes Sultaniye and Troy, Mycenaean pottery has been deposited as offerings for the deceased. Their quality and quantity in relation to the total number of offerings, both imported or locally produced, vary according to each site and the degree of interaction. Perhaps the Mycenaean elements are not astonishing and there is no adoption of the Mycenaean burial tradition, but they become more important when contrasted to the lack of any Hittite elements in the burials. Moreover, the existence of the built and tholos tombs may indicate the adoption of specific Mycenaean beliefs from parts of the local elite. However the presence of Mycenaean pots inside all kind of tombs and irrespective of status or wealth signifies that all strata of the local community accepted the symbolic significance of the Mycenaean items, whatever that may have been. These objects are selected and purposefully deposited along the deceased intermingled with the local ones. It is noteworthy that the Hittites funerary tradition is conspicuously poor and simple with the exception of the rituals followed for the royal burials (Gurney 1990, 137-8, 140). The Hittite burial context does not appear to have a special social, political or cultural significance, but for the Mycenaeans it was an important component of their identity and culture. This contrast between the Mycenaean and Hittite burial traditions is very important in order to understand the meanings articulated in the use of the Mycenaean funerary elements. Thus, this important difference in tradition between the two cultures emphasises the socio-political meaning attributed to the burials in East Aegean- Western Anatolia, while the Mycenaean elements confirm this theory.

In this area it is clear that we are not dealing with Mycenaean immigrants expressing their ethnic identity. Instead we are looking at the symbolic use of Mycenaean goods that are thought not only as desirable, but more importantly as indicative of the socio-political meanings ascribed to them. It is important to highlight that this process had a local character and that it was expressed in various ways. There is a definite manifestation of a pro-Mycenaean trend in the burial context, which is magnified by the lack of an equivalent Hittite one. The mortuary arena was an open field, free of restrictions and control from the Hittite administration, where socio-political messages and symbolisms could be more easily transmitted. Hence, the pro-Mycenaean metaphors are clearly conveyed to the participants of the burial practices, becoming meaningful in their local cultural context (Tilley 1999, 9). These messages are embedded into the individual and collective memory, using mainly local and older elements along with new one, forming ultimately new long lasting traditions (Halbwachs 1992, 86), as in the case of the Bakla Tepe burials.

The Hittite textual evidence

Since the decipherment of the Hittite texts the identification of the *Ahhiyawa* term has become a debated issue. Its occurrence in the texts is frequently followed by the place name of *Millawanda*. Thus from the beginning scholars have equated *Ahhiyawa* with the Achaians, the Homeric name of the Mycenaeans and *Millawanda* with Miletos. However, this was mainly a result of a phonetic resemblance and other areas in Anatolia and Thrace have been suggested over the years. The bulk of the proposed

geographical positions for these place names are really exhaustive as Niemeier (1998, 20-5) has demonstrated. Today the only alternative that draws support is placing *Millawanda* at the Troad and *Ahhiyawa* at Thrace (Houwink ten Cate 1973, 148; Easton 1984, 34; Mellaart and Murray 1995, 97-8), since from the texts we hear that the first was a port and the latter was beyond the sea.

The importance of the *Ahhiyawa* name that occurs in more than 25 texts is that it belongs to a kingdom beyond the immediate reach of the Hittites and recognized to have a king of equal status to the Hittite king. This is particular clear in the Amurru treaty where the name of the *Ahhiyawa* was erased by the scribe, who thought it appropriate to include them and certainly recognized them as one of the key political players of that time alongside the Egyptians, the Assyrians and the Babylonians (KUB XXIII I IV 23). The *Ahhiyawa* play an active role in Western Anatolia according to the Hittite texts at least since the times of Tudhaliya I, LH IIIA1 in Aegean terms (late 15th or early 14th century BC) (Bryce 1999, 140-1; Manning 1999, 225-7), providing a *terminus post quem*, until the fall of the Hittite empire (c.1200 BC). Moreover, recently two parts of a single text were put together revealing the geography of Western Anatolia, supporting the equation of *Millawanda* with Miletos. Following this development Hawkins (1998, 30-1) discovered a relief at Karabel confirming the above hypothesis by setting the limits of the Mira kingdom and consequently the position of *Millawanda*. Thus the original thought about the equation of *Ahhiyawa* with the Mycenaeans and *Millawanda* with Miletos has recently gained general support (Bryce 1989a, 6-7; Gurney 1990, 21; Taylour 1995, 158; Hawkins 1998, 20; Niemeier 1998, 37, 45). The Hittite conquest of *Millawanda* is mentioned in these texts, dated c. 1300 BC, whilst the appearance of a strong fortification in the end of the LH IIIA2 period at Miletos of Hittite style, corresponds well to the previous dating and textual reference.

The *Ahhiyawa* issue has monopolized the interest as far as the textual information for Western Anatolia is concerned. Thus, there is other interesting evidence supplied by the Hittite documents. First of all the island of Lesbos has been repeatedly reported in the tablets, known as Lazpa, and identified by almost all scholars. It seems that the island on its own was recognized as one political entity not unlike the rest of the Western Anatolian polities.

Nonetheless, the information provided for the Western Anatolia and its political structure are quite revealing. Although references concerning raids in the Arzawan territory are reported since the times of Hattusili I's reign (late 17th century BC), from the reign of Tudhaliya I (late 15th or early 14th century BC) and until the fall of the Hittite empire all Hittite kings had to deal with organized military operations in Western Anatolia. The unrests and rebellions were frequent causing important distractions in the Hittite affairs especially with the Syrian states and Egypt. Nevertheless, Western Anatolia had a strategic importance for the Hittites being quite close to their homeland.

During the 14th and 13th century BC several Western Anatolian states are found in the Hittite texts such as the Lukka Lands, identified with Classical Lycia, Mira, Arzawa, Seha River Land and *Wilusa*, equated with the Homeric Ilion i.e. the Troad (Niemeier 1999, 142-3; Easton *et al.* 2002, 94-101). It seems that Western Anatolia was politically fragmented, where a number of polities coexisted, most probably not unlike the political situation in the western coast of the Aegean. After the first dynamic Hittite intervention in the region by Tudhaliya I there was an immediate response with the formation of an anti-Hittite confederacy known as the *Assuwa* coalition by 22 states (Güterbock 1986, 40; Bryce 1989b, 308; 1999, 134-6; Vasilikou 1995, 389; Cline 1996, 145; Niemeier 1999, 145). From the conflict the Hittites won and dissolved this coalition, which never managed to be re-established, reducing these polities to vassal states. From that period on there were occasional cooperation and conflict among the Western Anatolian polities (Bryce 1999, 247). It also seems that in one of the rebellions against the Hittites, Arzawa, whose capital at Apasa is equated with Ephesos, at least for some time had managed to acquire its independence as the correspondence found at Amarna reveals (Gurney 1990, 22; Manning 1999, 227-8). In most of these autonomous efforts the *Ahhiyawans* seem to play a central role by acting directly or indirectly and causing considerable problems to the Hittites who complain in a number of their letters (Bryce 1999, 209-12, 244-6, 321-4). The *Ahhiyawan* activities in Western Anatolia ranging from *Millawanda* to *Wilusa* were not left unanswered by the Hittites. There seems that no direct conflict existed between the two powers, but the Hittites responded militarily in both cases and took over the areas. Furthermore, the existence of an embargo against the *Ahhiyawan* ships on Syria-Palestine coast under Hittite control in the 13th century is highly probable (Cline 1991a, 7-9), indicating the degree of measures taken against them.

Apart from the information related to the political context in Western Anatolia there is an important issue that emerges. The character of the *Assuwa* confederacy and whether a similar case could have taken place in the Greek mainland.

The *Assuwa* confederacy is a very interesting response to a specific historical moment. This political coalition of several polities must be stressed that took place when a common great threat appeared. It was an existential reaction since it represented an action of political independence against the Hittite hegemony. The polities must have had their conflicts over interests and borders, but at the time of need they cooperated. The result of its clash with the Hittites was the demolition of the coalition, an example that was not followed for rest of the LBA III in

Western Anatolia. An interesting historical parallel can be found in the same area several centuries later during the Ionian Revolt, 499-494 BC, against the Persians. Again several Greek city states both in Western Anatolia and East Aegean islands formed a confederacy in order to oppose the Persian rule. In this case political and military help was sought from mainland Greek polities, since they were recognized as sharing the same ethnic identity. Although Sparta was asked for help, only Athens and Eretria sent minor forces. However, this help did not play a central role in the revolt, which was crashed by the Persians. Few years later a similar coalition was formed by 31 independent city-states in the Greek mainland to oppose the Persian threat in 480-479 BC, only that in this case the confederacy was successful.

Although from these three examples the last two could be considered anachronistic they can give us some useful general ideas. All three examples are individual events to specific external threats with short lifespan, while none seems to have pre-existed and none followed thereafter. An exception, in a way, is the latest example from which the Delian League emerged, including some, but not all the initial members of the coalition. Yet again the original basic aim of the Delian League was none other than the repulse of the Persians from the Aegean and revenge (Bury and Meiggs 1992, 203). For the advocates of the Mycenaean confederacy and the situation described in the Iliad it becomes apparent that it remains a theoretical and fictional structure. No contemporary or later historical parallel of such a condition can be given in order to justify such a hypothesis. The only possible exception would have been the existence of a mercenary army financed by Mycenaean and Western Anatolian polities. A Mycenaean polity coalition could have taken place only in order to deal with a common threat, but it is highly unlikely to have been long lasting and have undertaken overseas enterprizes of the scale described in the Iliad by Homer.

Discussion

The East Aegean-Western Anatolia should not be seen just as a field of conflict between the Mycenaeans and the Hittites. At the same time it should not be considered as a mere bridge between East and West as Greaves (2007, 10-1) has correctly argued for Anatolia in a wider scale. East Aegean-Western Anatolia is a region with its own cultural characteristics and traditions with close interaction and relations with both the Greek mainland and Central Anatolia. The numerous revolts of the Western Anatolian polities emphasize their desire to be autonomous rather than mere Hittite vassal states. From the texts we have positive evidence that the *Ahhiyawans* helped them in a number of occasions with different ways. The Mycenaean remains in the East Aegean-Western Anatolia mark the close interaction between this area and the Greek mainland. Thus, they allow us to accept the *Ahhiyawa* equation with the Mycenaeans.

It has been noted earlier that the lack of standardization, at least in the pottery tradition, with the Hittite prototypes is the first hint for the cultural autonomy manifested in Western Anatolia beyond the texts. At the same time there is more concrete evidence that gives us deeper insights in the socio-political processes especially in the northern part of the East Aegean-Western Anatolia, the burial context. Most importantly there is a symbolic meaning attributed to the burials, which does not exist in the Hittite hinterland. The funerary context appears to be significant throughout the Aegean during the later phase of LBA, suggesting a *koine* regarding this expression with social and cultural connotations. Furthermore, the new traditions that are formed in this period have a strong Mycenaean component in them. Thus, the use of Mycenaean elements in their mortuary expression is varied, but at the same time conscious and highly symbolic. This is expressed with elements of grave form and construction, rituals and/or offerings. This tradition appears to have a different appearance within the burial practices of each site across the Eastern Aegean-Western Anatolia, but at the same time there is a common underling theme. These differenced are expressed according to the local cultural context and the degree of interaction with the Mycenaean world. Both wealthy and less wealthy burials incorporated Mycenaean characteristics demonstrating their desire to imitate and express their preference for them. These metaphors are the main vehicle to formulate the memory and tradition, which are inetrxicably linked with individual and communal identity. Thus, the adoption of some of the Mycenaean mortuary beliefs and practices emphasizes the conscious expression of a shared identity. This identity is not ethnic, and in my opinion no Mycenaean physical presence should be expected, but rather a socio-cultural one. The message of the newly formed burial tradition is inextricably linked to the contemporary socio-political conditions. In other words they express their favour for the autonomous socio-political structures, like the ones attested in the Mycenaean polities. The new elements incorporated in their burial practices created a new tradition, which has a strong ideological manifestation of political autonomy versus the Hittite control.

The Mycenaean political structure comprised of a number of polities with a substantial size and power in the LH IIIA2-B period with close interaction and relations in the whole Aegean and beyond. However, for the Western Anatolian polities it was something more substantial and important than that. The Mycenaeans were not only a good partner in exchanges and trade, a friend in times of need, but most importantly a socio-political model. The Mycenaean intervention in Western Anatolia was desired and welcomed most probably in the form of alliances and mutual aid. Perhaps the best evidence is the fact that after the fall of the Hittite empire and during the LH IIIC period (12th century BC), the Mycenaean material continued to be found in the area, in some cases in larger quantities, something that cannot be argued for the Hittite cultural influence. It was a process of interaction and interrelation that continued thereafter without any politico-cultural obstacles. The East Aegean-Western Anatolia allows us to have a fuller appreciation of the socio-political processes that were taking place during the last centuries of the Late Bronze Age in the wider Aegean and Anatolian region. At the southern part of this region the socio-political elements of the Mycenaean mainland culture became the dominant tradition. In the northern part due to the more limited interaction with mainland Greece and the direct involvement of the Central Anatolian Hittites, only parts of the Mycenaean culture were incorporated into the local tradition. In this area it can be more easily demonstrated how the Mycenaean socio-political structures were perceived and how they influenced the local cultures through the introduction of new traditions.

References

Achilara, L., 1986. 'Ανασκαφική δραστηριότητα στα Ψαρά', *Τα Ψαρά*, 10-1.

Achilara, L., 1996. 'Mycenaean events from Psara', *Atti e Memorie del Secondo Congresso Internazionale di Micenologia*, E. de Miro, L. Godart and A. Sacconi (eds.), Rome, 1349-53.

Andreou, E. and Andreou, I., 2001. 'Η Ίμβρος στην Πρώιμη Εποχή του Χαλκού', *Αρχαιολογία και Τέχνες* 81, 143-6.

Barber, R.L.N., 1999. 'Μυκηναίοι στη Φυλακωπή;', *Η Περιφέρεια του Μυκηναϊκού Κόσμου*, Lamia, 315-20.

Bass, G.F., 1963. 'Mycenaean and Protogeometric tombs in the Halikarnassos peninsula', *American Journal of Archaeology* 67, 353-61.

Benzi, M., 1992. *Rodi e la Civiltà Micenea*, vol. 1-2. Rome.

Bernabò-Brea, L., 1976. *Il Poliochni Città Preistorica nell' Isola di Lemnos vol. II,1*, [Monografie della Scuola Arceologica di Atene e delle Mission Italiane in Oriente], Rome.

Blegen, C.W., Caskey, J.L. and Rawson, M., 1953. *Troy, The Sixth Settlement*, vol. III, part 1. Princeton.

Boysal, Y., 1967. 'New excavations in Caria', *Anadolu (Anatolia)* 11, 31-56.

Bridges, R.A.Jr., 1974. 'The Mycenaean tholos tomb at Kolophon', *Hesperia* 43, 264-6.

Bryce, T.R., 1989a. 'The nature of Mycenaean involvement in Western Anatolia', *Historia* 38, 1-21.

Bryce, T.R., 1989b. 'Ahhiyawans and Mycenaeans- an Anatolian viewpoint', *Oxford Journal of Archaeology* 8, 297-310.

Bryce, T., 1999. *The Kingdom of the Hittites*. Oxford.

Bury, J.B. and Meiggs, R., 1992. *A History of Greece*. London.

Cavanagh, W.G., 1978. 'A Mycenaean second burial custom?', *Bulletin of the Institute of Classical Studies* 25, 171-2.

Charitonidis, S.I., 1961/2a. 'Μάκαρα', *Αρχαιολογικόν Δελτίον* 17 *Χρονικά*, 265.

Charitonidis, S., 1961/2b. 'Ψαρά', *Αρχαιολογικόν Δελτίον* 17 *Χρονικά*, 266.

Cline, E.H., 1991a. 'A possible embargo against the Mycenaeans', *Historia* 40, 1-9.

Cline, E.H., 1991b. 'Hittite objects in the Bronze Age Aegean', *Anatolian Studies* 41, 133-43.

Cline, E.H., 1996. 'Aššuwa and the Achaeans, the 'Mycenaean' sword at the Hattušas and its possible implications', Annual of the British School at Athens 91, 137-51.

Davis, J.L. and Bennet, J., 1999. 'Making Mycenaeans, warfare, territorial expansion, and representations of the other in the Pylian kingdom', *Polemos*, [Aegaeum 19], R. Laffineur (ed.), Liège, 105-20.

Deger-Jalkotzy, S., 1999. 'Military prowess and social status in Mycenaean Greece', *Polemos*, [Aegaeum 19], R. Laffineur (ed.), Liège, 121-31.

Dickinson, O.T.P.K., 1992. *Η Προέλευση του Μυκηναϊκού Πολιτισμού*, A. Papadopoulos (trns.). Athens

Driessen, J., 1990. *An Early Destruction in the Mycenaean Palace at Knossos*. Leuven.

Driessen, J. and MacDonald, C., 1984. 'Some military aspects of the Aegean in the late fifteenth and early fourteenth centuries BC', *Annual of the British School at Athens* 79, 49-74.

Driessen, J. and Macdonald, C.F., 1997. *The Troubled Island- Minoan Crete Before and After the Santorini Eruption*, [Aegaeum 17], Liège.

Easton, D.F., 1984. 'Hittite history and the Trojan war', *The Trojan War- Its Historicity and Context*, L. Foxhall and J.K. Davies (eds.), Bristol, 23-44.

Easton, D.F., Hawkins, J.D., Sherratt, A.G. and Sherratt, E.S., 2002. 'Troy in recent perspective', *Anatolian Studies* 52, 75-109.

Erkanal, H., 1998. 'Geç tunç çağı', *Kazi Sonuçlari Toplantisi* 19, 401-17.

Erkanal, A. and Erkanal, H. 1986. 'A new archaeological excavation in Western Anatolia; Panaztepe', *Turkish Review Quaterly Digest*, 67-76.

Ersoy, Y.E., 1988. 'Finds from Menemen/Panaztepe in the Manisa museum', Annual of the British School at Athens 83, 55-82.

French, E., 2002. *Mycenae- Agamemnon's Capital*, Gloucestershire.

Furumark, A., 1950. 'The settlement at Ialysos and Aegean history c. 1550-1400 BC', Opuscula *Archaeologica* 6, 150-271.

Georgiadis, M., 2003. *The South-Eastern Aegean during the Mycenaean Period, Islands, landscape, death and ancestors,* [BAR International Series 1196], Oxford.

Georgiadis, M., 2004. 'Migration on Rhodes during the Mycenaean Period', *Journal of Mediterranean Archaeology and Archaeometry* 4.1, 34-48.

Georgiadis, M., (in press). 'The South-eastern Aegean at the end of the Bronze Age, A crossroads of interaction', *Forces of Transformation, The End of the Bronze Age in the Mediterranean*, Oxbow Books, Oxford.

Greaves, A.M., 2002. *Miletos- A History,* London.

Greaves, A.M., 2007. 'Trans-Anatolia, examining Turkey as a bridge between East and West', *Transanatolia, Anatolian Studies* 57, 1-15.

Greaves, A.M. and Helwing, B. 2001. 'Archaeology in Turkey, the Stone, Bronze and Iron Ages, 1997-1999', *American Journal of Archaeology* 105, 463-511.

Greaves, A.M. and Helwing, B., 2003. 'Archaeology in Turkey, the Stone, Bronze and Iron Ages, 2000', *American Journal of Archaeology* 107, 71-103.

Gurney, O.R., 1990. *The Hittites,* London.

Güterbock, H.G., 1986. 'Troy in Hittite texts? Wilusa, Ahhiyawa, and Hittite history', *Troy and the Trojan War*, Mellink M.J. (ed.), Bryn Mawr, 33-44.

Halbwachs, M., 1992. *On Collective Memory*, edited, translated and with an introduction by L.A. Coser, Chicago.

Hanfmann, G.M.A. and Waldbaum, J.C., 1968. 'Two Submycenaean vases and a tablet from Stratonikeia in Caria', *American Journal of Archaeology* 72, 51-6.

Hawkins, J.D., 1998. 'Tarkasnawa king of Mira 'Tarkondemos', Boğazköy sealings and Karabel', *Anatolian Studies* 48, 1-31.

Hood, S., 1981. *Excavations in Chios 1938-1955 Prehistoric Emporio and Ayio Gala* vol.1-2, [the British School of Archaeology at Athens, supplementary 15-6], Oxford.

Hope Simpson, R., 1965. *A Gazetteer and Atlas of Mycenaean Sites*, [Bulletin Supplement 16], London.

Hope Simpson, R., 2003. 'The Dodecanese and the Ahhiyawa question', *Annual of the British School at Athens* 98, 203-37.

Hope Simpson, R. and Lazenby, J.F., 1970. 'Notes from the Dodecanese ii', *Annual of the British School at Athens* 65, 47-77.

Houwink Ten Cate, P.H.J. 1973. 'Anatolian evidence for relations with the West in the Late Bronze Age', *Bronze Age Migrations in the Aegean- Archaeological and Linguistic Problems in Greek Prehistory*, R.A. Crossland and A. Birchall (eds.), London, 141-61.

Izmir Region Excavations and Research Programs (IRERP) 2000. 'Excavations at Bakla Tepe', visited on 7/2/03, http://www.geocities.com/irerp_tr/frames.html.

Kanta, A., 1980. *The Late Minoan III Period in Crete, A Survey of Sites, Pottery and their Distribution*, [SIMA 58], Göteborg.

Karantzali, E., 2001. *The Mycenaean Cemetery at Pylona on Rhodes*, [BAR International Series 988], Oxford.

Kilian, K., 1990. 'Mycenaean colonization, norm and variety', *Greek Colonists and Native Populations- Proceedings of the First Australian Congress of Classical Archaeology held in honour of Emeritus Professor A.D. Trendall*, J.-P. Descœudres (ed.). Oxford, 445-67.

Korfmann, M., 1986. 'Beşik Tepe, new evidence for the period of the Trojan sixth and seventh settlements', *Troy and the Trojan War*, Mellink M.J. (ed.), Bryn Mawr, 17-28.

Lamb, W., 1936. *Excavations at Thermi in Lesbos*, Cambridge.

Macdonald, C.F., 1985. *The Relationship of Crete and Mainland Greece to the Islands of the South Aegean During the Late Bronze Age,* Unpublished PhD thesis, Oxford.

Manning, S.W., 1999. *A Test of Time*, Oxford.

Marketou, S., 1980. 'Λέρος', *Αρχαιολογικόν Δελτίον* 35 Χρονικά, 557.

Mee, C., 1978. 'Aegean trade and settlement in Anatolia in the Second Millennium B.C.', *Anatolian Studies* 28, 121-56.

Mee, C., 1982. *Rhodes in the Bronze Age, An Archaeological Survey*, Warminster.

Mee, C., 1988. 'A Mycenaean thalassocracy in the Eastern Aegean?', *Problems in Greek Prehistory*, E.B. French and K.A. Wardle (eds.), Bristol, 301-6.

Mee, C., 1998. 'Anatolia and the Aegean in the Late Bronze Age', *The Aegean and the Orient in the Second Millennium*, [Aegaeum 18], E.C. Cline and D. Harris-Cline (eds.), Liège, 137-48.

Melas, E.M., 1985. *The Islands of Karpathos, Saros and Kasos in the Neolithic and Bronze Age*, [SIMA 68], Göteborg.

Melas, M., 1988. 'Exploration in the Dodecanese, new prehistoric and Mycenaean finds', *Annual of the British School at Athens* 83, 283-311.

Mellaart, J. and Murray, A., 1995. *Beycesultan* vol. III Part II. Oxford.

Messineo, G., 1997. 'Gli scavi di Efestia a Lemno, tradizione Micenea nella civiltà Tirrenica', *Studi Micenei ed Egeo-Anatolici* 39, 241-52.

Mountjoy, P.A., 1998. 'The East Aegean–West Anatolian Interface in the Late Bronze Age, Mycenaeans and the kingdom of Ahhiyawa', *Anatolian Studies* 48, 33-68.

Mountjoy, P.A., 1999. 'The destruction of Troia Vih', *Studia Troica* 9, 253-93.

Mylonas, G.E., 1966. *Mycenae and the Mycenaean Age,* Princeton.

Niemeier, W.-D., 1998. 'The Mycenaeans in Western Anatolia and the problem of the origins of the Sea Peoples', *Mediterranean Peoples in Transition- Thirteen to Early Tenth Centuries BCE*, S. Gitin, A. Mazar and E. Stern (eds.), Jerusalem, 17-65.

Niemeier, W.-D., 1999. 'Mycenaeans and Hittites in war in Western Asia Minor', *Polemos*, R. Laffineur (ed.), [Aegaeum 19], Liège, 141-56.

Philimonos, M., 1996. 'Τήλος, Μεγάλο Χωριό', *Αρχαιολογικόν Δελτίον* 51 Χρονικά, 693-7.

Popham, M., 1980. 'Cretan sites occupied between c.1450-1400 BC', *Annual of the British School at Athens* 75, 163-7.

Postgate, J.N., 2007. 'The ceramics of centralisation and dissolution, a case study from Rough Cilicia', *Transanatolia, Anatolian Studies* 57, 141-50.

Preston, L., 1999. 'Mortuary practices and the negotiation of social identities at LM II Knossos', *Annual of the British School at Athens* 94, 131-43.

Preston, L., 2004. 'A mortuary perspective on political changes in Late Minoan II-IIIB Crete', *American Journal of Archaeology* 108, 321-48.

Rutter, J.B., 1993. 'Review of Aegean prehistory ii, the Prepalatial Bronze Age of the southern and central Greek mainland', *American Journal of Archaeology* 97, 745-97.

Schachner, A. and Meriç, R., 2000. 'Ein Stempelsiegel des späten 2 Jahrtausends v. chr. aus Metropolis in Ionien', *Study Micenei ed Egeo-Anatolici* 42, 85-102.

Schallin, A.-L., 1993. *Islands Under Influence, The Cyclades in the Late Bronze Age and the Nature of Mycenaean Presence*, [SIMA 111], Jonsered.

Shelmerdine, C.W., 1997. 'Review of Aegean prehistory vi, the palatial Bronze Age of the southern and central Greek mainland', *American Journal of Archaeology* 101, 537-85.

Skerlou, E., 1996. 'Περίχωρα της πόλης Κω', *Αρχαιολογικόν Δελτίον* 51 Χρονικά, 689-92.

Skerlou, E., 1997. 'Περίχωρα της πόλης Κω', *Αρχαιολογικόν Δελτίον* 52 Χρονικά, 1112.

Spencer, N., 1995. 'Early Lesbos between East and West, a 'grey area' of Aegean archaeology', *Annual of the British School at Athens* 90, 269-305.

Sperling, J., 1991. 'The last phase of Troy VI and Mycenaean expansion', *Studia Troica* 1, 155-7.

Taylour, W., 1995. *The Mycenaeans*, London.

Thompson, D., 2007. 'At the crossroads, prehistoric settlement in the Maeander valley', *Transanatolia, Anatolian Studies* 57, 87-99.

Tilley, C., 1999. *Metaphor and Material Culture*, Oxford.

Treuil, R., Darcque, P., Poursat, J.-C. and Touchais, G., 1996. *Οι Πολιτισμοί του Αιγαίου*, translated by A.P. Touchais, Athens.

Vasilikou, N., 1995. *Ο Μυκηναϊκός Πολιτισμός,* Athens.

Vermeule, E., 1972. *Greece in the Bronze Age*, Chicago.

Watrous, L.V., 1993. 'Cretan relations with the Aegean and the Late Bronze Age', *Wace and Blegen*, C. Zerner, P. Zerner and J. Winder (eds.), Amsterdam, 81-90.

Wiener, M.H., 1984. 'Crete and the Cyclades in LM I, the tale of the conical cups', *The Minoan Thalassocracy- Myth and Reality*, R. Hägg and N. Marinatos (eds.), Stockholm, 17-25.

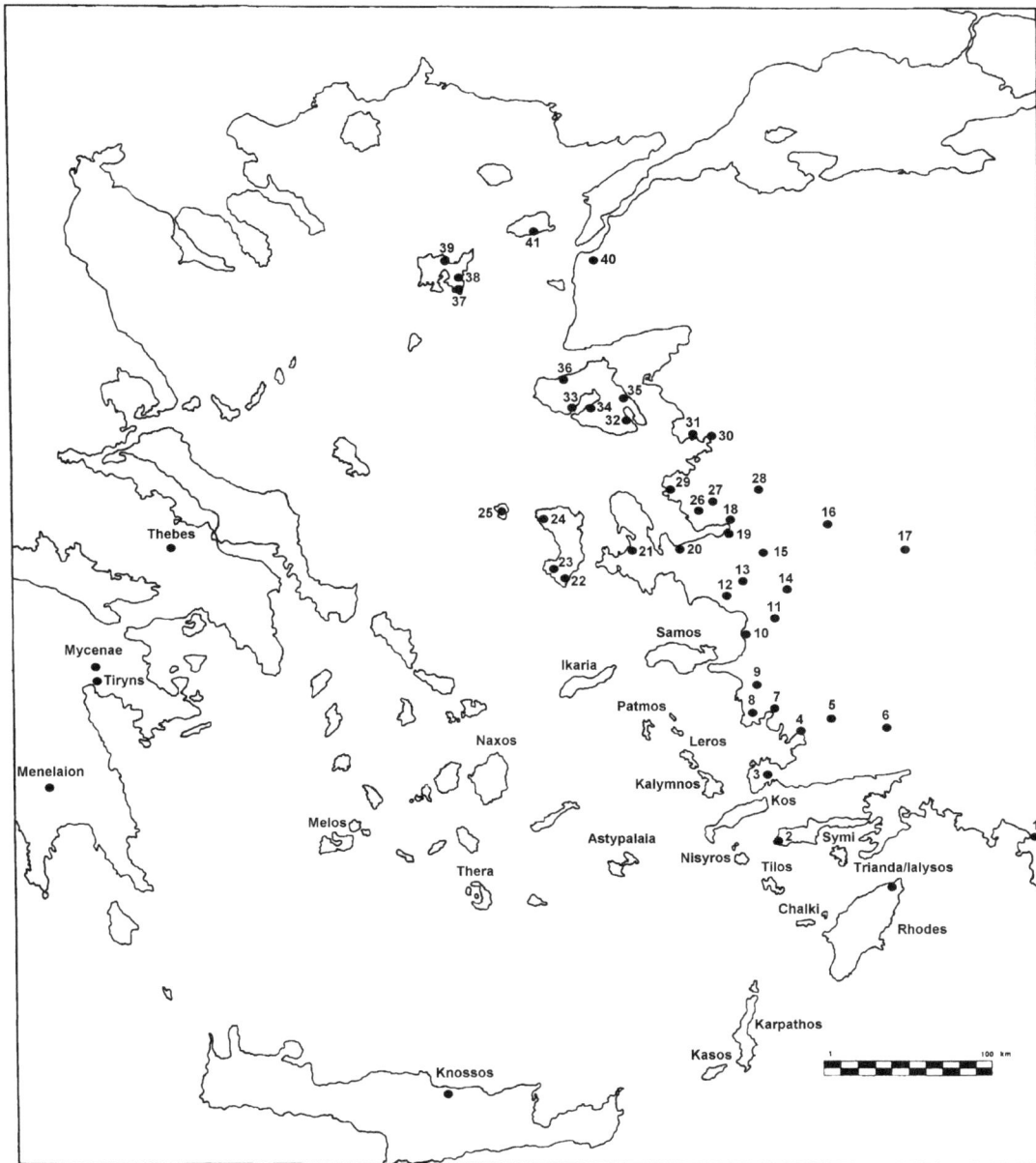

Figure 1. Sites mentioned in text with emphasis to East Aegean- Western Anatolia

Keys to Map

1	Telmessos		22	Emporio
2	Cape Krio/Knidos		23	Kato Phana
3	Müskebi		24	Volissos
4	Iasos		25	Archontiki
5	Mylasa		26	Panaztepe
6	Stratinikaia		27	Larisa
7	Akbük		28	Çerkes Sultaniye
8	Didyma		29	Phocaia
9	Miletos		30	Elaia
10	Kuşadasi		31	Pitane
11	Ayasoluk/Ephesos		32	Perama
12	Kolophon		33	Makara
13	Bakla Tepe		34	Kourtir
14	Tire-Ahmetler		35	Thermi
15	Metropolis		36	Antissa
16	Sardis		37	Koukonisi
17	Gavurtepe		38	Poliochni
18	Smyrna		39	Ifestia
19	Izmir		40	Troy- Beşik Tepe
20	Liman Tepe/Clazomenai		41	Imvros
21	Erythrai			

Memories of place.
Bronze Age rock art and landscape in West Norway

Melanie Wrigglesworth

Introduction

In this paper, I will discuss social memory in relation to rock art, based on a case study from West Norway (Fig.1). Rock art dated to the Late Mesolithic/the Neolithic (6400–1700 BC) and the Bronze Age (1700–500 BC) will be discussed. There are two traditions of rock art in Scandinavia, "hunter's rock art", dated to the Stone Age, and "agrarian rock art", dated to the Bronze Age and Early Iron Age (500-1 BC). Here, the terms Stone Age rock art and Bronze Age rock art will be used. Stone Age motifs include animals such as red deer, elk, reindeer and whales, as well as boats, anthropomorphic figures and geometrical motifs. They are associated with hunter-gatherer groups and are often linked to shamanism and animism. Bronze Age motifs include cup marks, ships, human representations, objects such as axes and swords in particular, animals such as dogs, bulls and horses, and geometrical designs e.g. rings and concentric rings. This type of rock art is traditionally associated with an agrarian population and interpreted in terms of ritual, religion and cosmology.

Social memory

Cultural identity defines a community or group, and that identity is based on the history of the group. In other words, the past is part of our identity in the present. We are what and who we are partly because society shapes us, so that we have a cultural or social identity. Rock art sites were reused and are places where the past in terms of earlier carvings would have existed in the present. Our experience of the present depends on our knowledge of the past (Connerton 1989). Social memory is '(…) an expression of collective experience, social memory identifies a group, giving it a sense of its past and defining its aspirations for the future' (Fentress and Wickham 1992, 25). Several types of memory can be distinguished, personal memory, which is related to personal experiences in the past; cognitive memory, remembering knowledge that one does not need to have experienced; and 'habit-memory', remembering through reproducing a performance or action, such as swimming or riding a bike (Connerton 1989, 22-4). These types of memory are all linked to individuals – this is how individuals remember. Memory is both collective and personal, it is subjective and individual, but is also structured by language, images, collectively held ideas and experiences shared with other people, effectively making memory social (Fentress and Wickham 1992, 7). Memory must also be transmitted and articulated in order to be social, and methods of transmitting are through speech, rituals, body language (Fentress and Wickham 1992, 47). Social memory is closely linked to both personal and group identity; although experience shapes a person's memories and personal identity, groups are a stable frame for identity and memory, providing individuals with frameworks where memories are localised (Fentress and Wickham 1992, 37). Memory has an inherent dualism in terms of function. It can be used for an accurate representation of the past, as well as for creating a 'usable' past (Wertsch 2002, 31). This implies that one function of memory is to create a past. The creation of a usable past means creating a collective identity, based on experience and tradition. Social memory reflects the social framework of a particular group and is subjective in the sense that different groups or communities have different collective memories (Wertsch 2002, 40-5).

In order to create a collective identity, determining who belongs to that identity is necessary (Straub 2002, 68), and this can be done by emphasising cultural identity. Codes and symbols are part of the cultural 'language', and have been accumulated over time (Dodgshon 1998, 169). As mentioned above, memory is composed of images, speech, experiences, and emotions. Images in particular are metaphors, they contain information that persons with the same cultural identity can make sense of. Metaphors involve taking a term from one frame of reference and using it within a different frame of reference (Tilley 1999, 4). The metaphor links individuals and groups in that it refers to specific cultural knowledge, hence metaphors may not be understood by someone who is not a member of a specific cultural group (Tilley 1999, 9). Identity and metaphors are thus closely linked, and this creates a basis for constructing a collective experience and social memory. Like metaphors, images have significant cultural connotations, but in order to be understood by everyone they have to be simple. Complex images are proportionately difficult to understand (Fentress and Wickham 1992; Bradley 1997). In the case of rock art, this would mean that simple motifs could have contained information available to a larger group, while complex motifs may have

contained specialised information only understood by a small number of people.

According to Connerton (1989), there are two types of social practice, inscribing practices, where memory is stored in books, computers etc, and incorporating practices, where memory is stored through bodily activity or presence (Connerton 1989, 72-3). The latter is associated with commemorative practices and ceremonies that are performative. Social memory is found in commemorative ceremonies, such as rituals, where repetition accentuates continuity with the past (Connerton 1989, 44-9). Rituals are a formalised method of remembering or commemoration. Traditions are created and upheld by ritual, however, at some point, the origins of a particular tradition may be forgotten, or the tradition changes, without people being aware of the process (Bell 1992, 118). Rock art can be seen as an inscribed practice, as the images are carved or painted on stone. However, making rock art or performing rituals at a rock art site are incorporating practices. Body language is, accordingly, part of an incorporating practice and helps communicate social memory. So, the body and social and personal memory are connected - memory connects us to our bodies and the body connects us to the world in which we live (Fentress and Wickham 1992, 39). Social memory says who and why we are, and creates as well as maintains identity.

Landscape, memory and monuments

Social memory cannot exist without reference to a specific spatial framework (Halbwachs 1992). Memory is preserved by referring to the material world, so that mental spaces refer to the material spaces that a group occupies (Connerton 1989; Fentress and Wickham 1992, 37; Taçon 1994; Ingold 2000, 122-3; Stewart and Strathern 2003, 4-5). The landscape consists of places and topographical features imbued with meaning and linked to memory. Personal memories are often tied to specific places, and memories may be triggered by places or actions. Memory tends to be organised around places and sensory experience, and may leave traces in the landscape (Halbwachs 1992; Misztal 2003, 16-7); consequently, the landscape includes both collective and personal memory. Some places have personal significance on an individual level, while other places are significant on a collective or communal level. For instance, a rock art site that has been used for centuries would presumably have been important to a community, while simultaneously creating memories for individuals taking part in any ceremonies or rituals taking place at the site. Memory is materialised through monuments, ideology, through bodily performances and is an inherent part of the life-world. It is materialised through monuments such as cairns and rock art sites, as well as old settlement sites. The landscape can thus be seen as a materialisation of memory, it also constitutes the life-world, the world in which people live and perceive.

Monuments are about communication and commemoration. The term 'monument' comes from Latin 'memore', to remind (Bradley 1993, 2002). Through monuments, the past exists in the present and in the future. Monuments are eternal and timeless, and as such are fundamental in the transmission and maintenance of social memory. They are also a means of communication - ideas, cultural and social identity can be communicated through them. However, neither their meaning nor their form is fixed, the meaning of a monument may change drastically from the time of its construction (Bradley 1993; 2000; Barrett 1999; Edmonds 1999), and monuments can be rebuilt or changed. New ideas are legitimised through references to the past, and by referring to the past, traditions are upheld or given new meaning; however, traditions may also be constructed in order to create continuity where none existed

(Edmonds 1999). Accordingly, the past is essential in legitimising ideas and traditions.

Social memory expressed through Bronze Age rock art

Rock art sites generally show stylistic and chronological variation, indicating modification over time, stylistically different motifs, changing techniques, re-carving older images, or superimposed images. Different sites have different points of completion - some have only two or three images, possibly made within a short period; at other sites there are large numbers of stylistically different images that have been created over a very long period, perhaps centuries. This means that rock art sites were part of life in prehistory, and so they may be places of memory.

Rock art sites are prime sources of social memory because they consist of images carved in stone and are permanent places in the landscape. The images might have contained stories related to history, cosmology and cosmogony; although we do not know what the images actually mean, they must have been accompanied by words and actions - performances, the act of making new carvings, and so on. The narratives that accompanied the images could well have been cosmological stories, or stories about how the world came into being. These stories would have helped to create a sense of identity and community, the essence of social memory. So, rock art sites constitute places that are fixed in the landscape, places that people could return to. Thus the sites would become fixed in peoples' lives, and so would the events that took place at the sites. The images would have been a visual reminder of stories, as well as a visual accompaniment to recited stories, poems and songs. As such, rock art sites would have constituted nuclei of social memory, places that reinforced personal and group identity. Such places could accordingly have served as reminders of communal history.

Places of memory, Hardanger, West Norway

The area known as Hardanger has a large concentration of Bronze Age rock art, mainly concentrated along the Hardanger fjord system (Fig.2). The landscape is hilly and is characterised by narrow strips of land between the fjord and the mountains. The rock art sites are spread on outcrops and boulders along the fjord, near the sea, between approximately 10 and 40 metres above sea level. Most cup-mark sites are however located on the steep hillsides, near paths leading up to the mountains or in the mountains. The majority of rock art in Hardanger can be dated to the Bronze Age; only two sites have been dated to the Stone Age (Larsen 1972; Bakka 1973; Mandt 2002). However, as their location in the landscape is identical to that of the Bronze Age art, they will be included here. I have singled out a number of sites that have certain similarities in terms of location and seven sites comprising eight panels will be discussed. This does not mean that other sites that do not have these qualities can not be interpreted in terms of social memory.

The sites are located to the north of the Hardanger fjord; all are found at the foot of a hill or large outcrop, and the rock art is found on vertical panels. In general, Western Norwegian sites are located on more or less horizontal or slanted surfaces or boulders, so that vertical panels are unusual; accordingly, it is interesting to find seven such sites over a relatively small distance and along the same coastline. These sites have several points in common apart from the vertical surface. They are located at the foot of medium-sized hills or large outcrops, close to the sea. The dominating motifs are boats (of a type generally dated to the Early Bronze Age, although this does not apply to all sites) and the oldest carvings appear to be located at the top of the panel, while later carvings are found in the lower part near the ground.

The Early Bronze Age type of boat, classified as type A1 by Mandt (1991), has a square hull, flat keel and the stern is either straight or at a slight angle. B1 type boats are also found at some of the sites, this type is identical to A1, except that it has no gunwale and is most likely a variety of the A1 boat. The A1 boat is commonly found at a small number of sites in Western and Central Norway, and is similar to boats dated to the Stone Age (Sognnes 1987; Mandt 1991). Consequently, this type has been seen as a development of the Stone Age design and has been dated to the very beginning of the Bronze Age. A1 type boats have been recorded in the burial chamber in a barrow, Mjeltehaugen, Northwest Norway, dated to the Early Bronze Age (Mandt 1983; Linge 2005; 2007). Rock carvings are notoriously difficult to date; however, contemporary decorated bronze artefacts as well as shoreline data may indicate an approximate date (Kaul 1998; Sognnes 2003; Ling 2005). Here, Mandt's chronological typology is used (Larsen 1972; Mandt 1991).

In order to understand the possible link between rock art, landscape and memory, I have carried out a landscape analysis, focusing on variables such as proximity to water and other lines of communication, and visibility to and from the site. I have also considered whether there is a continuity of place, i.e whether the place has been used over a long period of time and consequently whether it may have been significant over a long period.

Rykkje

The site is located at the foot of a hill, ending in a small cliff near a red deer track (Gjerde 1998, 71). Only one carving is recorded at Rykkje, a depiction of a deer or reindeer. The site is accessible; it is visible from a large area and there is a good view of the fjord. Bronze Age carvings, now lost, were found in the area in the early 20th century (Larsen 1972).

Vangdal

The site (Fig.3) consists of three panels, two of which are found at the top and the foot of a large outcrop. The third panel is placed at some distance from the outcrop, and is of uncertain date. The highest panel is Vangdal 2, situated precariously on the edge of the outcrop. The motifs are deer, human representations and geometrical designs. Based on shoreline data as well as typology, the carvings were produced in the Stone Age, and may be Late Mesolithic or Neolithic (Bakka 1973; Gjerde 1998; 2002). Vangdal 1 is located at the foot of the outcrop, and consists of A1/B1 type boats, suggesting an Early Bronze Age date; and possibly that the carvings were made within a relatively short period. One boat appears to have been re-carved, indicating repeated visits to the site. The outcrop is a dominating feature in the landscape and is visible from a considerable distance from the fjord. The outcrop does not face the sea directly. With a higher shoreline than at present, Vangdal would have been a good landing place for boats.

Fonnaland

The site (Fig.4) consists of three boats of general Bronze Age date, most likely Late Bronze Age. The panel is located at the foot of a small hill that ends in a cliff, facing the water and has a wide view of the fjord. It is accessible and visible from the fjord.

Linga

The site (Fig.5) is located on a small outcrop that does not face the water directly. More than 70 ships are depicted on the rock, most of which are Mandt's type A1, dating the site to the Early Bronze Age. The remaining ships can be dated to the beginning of the Late Bronze Age. The outcrop is small and less dominant in the landscape; although the place would have been visible from a distance, the outcrop itself might not be as easy to spot. The site is accessible and has a panoramic view of the fjord.

Berge

The site (Fig.6) is located at the foot of a small mountain with a panoramic view of the fjord, which it faces. The small mountain is visible from a great distance and is a dominant landscape feature. Three B1 type boats have been documented, about four metres above ground and set slightly apart from the other images. The remaining boats are Late Bronze Age types; some may possibly be dated to the Early Iron Age (500-1 BC). A small excavation in front of the panel revealed deposits of sand and charcoal, which were radiocarbondated to the Early Iron Age (Lødøen 2005, 203). This does not necessarily indicate the date of the rock art, although some carvings could well have been made in this period. The site is easily accessible; based on the excavation and shoreline data (Gjerde 1998; 2002; Lødøen 2005), it is likely that at times the site was only accessible by boat.

Hammarhaug

This site (Fig.7) is located at the foot of a small hill, and the location in the landscape is identical to Berge, although the view from the site is more restricted as it is partially blocked by rising ground. The site faces the sea, which would have been very close to the hill. The motifs are several boats of Late Bronze Age date.

Halhjem

This site (Fig.8) is not located in the Hardangerfjord area, but further to the north in the adjoining Bjørnefjord. I have included it here because the panel is vertical and its landscape setting is similar to the sites mentioned above. The site is located at the foot of a very small hill. The location in the landscape differs from the other sites in some respects – the hill is close to the sea, but the rock art was made at a point from which the sea is not visible, a short walk from the shore. Although the site is accessible, the ground slopes down towards the panel, effectively creating a basin. There is no view from the site and it is not visible until one gets quite close, so that the site has a more private character. The motifs are boats, cup-marks and rings of Late Bronze Age date, possibly Early Iron Age. This site emulates the characteristics of the other sites further north, and this panel and location were chosen because the panel had the required physical attributes.

The seven sites presented above have specific properties in terms of structure, motifs, and location in the landscape. There are no other sites with the same type of motifs on horizontal or slanted panels north of the Hardangerfjord. There is no shortage of suitable outcrops, indicating that for some reason, rock carvings had to be made on vertical surfaces in this particular area. No sites south of the fjord have A1/B1 type boats, and their location in the landscape is slightly different (Larsen 1972). Based on the early dates of this type of ship (Mandt 1991), three of the seven sites are the earliest Bronze Age sites in the area. As there are two Stone Age rock art sites in visible and partially accessible locations in the area, a possible interpretation is that the locations for the Bronze Age carvings were chosen because of the older carvings. As both Stone Age sites are vertical, choosing structurally similar sites could have been one way of linking to the past.

The stylistic variation at the seven sites also indicates that they were repeatedly visited. Sometimes, several hundred years may have passed before new carvings were made, as is the case at Berge. In the case of Vangdal 1 and 2, a continuity of place from the Stone Age to the Bronze Age is evident. This also applies to Linga and Berge, where the presence of A1 type boats and Late Bronze Age ships indicate that the sites were used over a long period. At Rykkje, the now lost Bronze Age carvings would indicate some continuity of place here as well. Fonnaland, Hammarhaug and Halhjem are different; based on style, they were created in the Late Bronze Age and it is difficult to say whether these sites were used over a similarly long period. However, I suggest that there is a continuity of place at these sites, based on the properties of the places and the structural similarities to Rykkje, Vangdal, Berge and Linga. Although the places may not have been used in the Early Bronze Age as far as making rock art is concerned, they might have had significance in terms of associations with stories and myths, and images were carved at a later stage. Alternatively, these places came into existence because they were structurally similar to Vangdal, Berge, and Linga, and were thus associated with whatever stories and powers that were believed to exist at those sites.

Thus, a possible interpretation is that Vangdal 1, Linga and Berge were the first Bronze Age sites in the area, copying or recreating the older sites Rykkje and Vangdal 2. The sites were re-used throughout the Bronze Age, although stylistic variation and the number of figures indicate that rock art was not made continually. People may still have come to these places in order to perform rituals, existing images might have been painted, or new parts added to old images (Wahlgren 2002). In the case of Berge, most images were actually made in the Late Bronze Age. During the Late Bronze Age, new sites were created at Fonnaland, Hammarhaug and Halhjem; like the Early Bronze Age sites, they have vertical panels and have the same location in the landscape, i.e. they are visible and accessible, they are close to the sea and with the exception of Halhjem, there is a good view of the surrounding landscape from the sites. It could well be that in these cases it was believed that rock art could only be made in places that were similar to the places chosen by the ancestors. Thus, the Stone Age sites structured the location of the Early Bronze Age sites, which in turn structured the later sites. Throughout the Bronze Age and perhaps in the Early Iron Age as well, people returned to these places and eventually, the carvings from the Early Bronze Age would have been perceived as images from the past, created by the ancestors.

Rock art and social memory

The case study indicates that in the Hardangerfjord area, the sites were places that people returned to over a long period, in order to make new rock art and to perform rituals. The sites that can be dated to the Early Bronze Age have the same location in the landscape as the sites from the Stone Age and in the case of Vangdal, the Stone Age and Bronze Age panels are found on the same outcrop. Later, new places that were similar to older and established places were created. At these sites, memory is preserved through a specific location in the landscape and to some extent through the choice of motifs - relatively simple boats were preferred. The sites discussed above demonstrate various practices - perhaps different incorporating practices. Established places were reused, by carving new images on the same panels, or by creating new panels near existing ones or in similar locations. The sites were already significant and this could be seen as a way of tapping into that significance. Social memory is thus expressed through repeated visits, reusing panels at existing sites and *recreating* sites.

Rock art was not placed randomly in the landscape, it was located in places that were significant to people in the Bronze Age. Some of those locations were at spectacular or dominant features in the landscape, as the sites in the case study demonstrate. The sites discussed above are all located in open and accessible places, near water and lines of communication. They were public, located in highly visible places between the sea and the mountains. The rituals that included making rock carvings may thus have been communal or collective, aimed at a large group of people, and could have commemorated specific events in the past, creating and upholding group identity. Making rock art near older rock art or imitating the properties of earlier sites would have been a means of connecting with the past and legitimising social positions within the group. The motifs are simple and the information they contained could thus have been available to a group sharing the same cultural identity and the same past. A possible interpretation is that the past was instrumental in creating and upholding the social and cultural fabric of the community.

Reused sites are part of an incorporating social practice, where social memory is maintained through ritual (Connerton 1989). Rock art can be seen as both an inscribing and incorporating practice - the sites are physical representations of the past as well as places where memory was transmitted and upheld. All rock art sites can potentially be seen as the physical remains of rituals, where the transmission of social memory through ritual performance may have been one element. In this sense, social memory is about preserving the world. By reusing sites and creating new sites that are similar to the older sites, it would have been possible to share or create a common identity and ideology as well as legitimise social positions. Rock art could thus have been part of a cultural construction of memory.

References

Bakka, E., 1973. 'Om alderen på veideristningane', *Viking*, 151-87.

Barrett, J.C., 1999. 'Chronologies of landscape', *The Archaeology and Anthropology of Landscape*, P. Ucko and R. Layton (eds.), London, 21-30.

Bell, C., 1992. *Ritual theory, ritual practice*, Oxford.

Bradley, R., 1993. *Altering the Earth*, [Society of Antiquaries of Scotland Monograph Series 8], Edinburgh.

Bradley, R., 1997. *Rock Art and the Prehistory of Atlantic Europe*, London.

Bradley, R., 2000. *An Archaeology of Natural Places*, London.

Bradley, R., 2002. *The Past in Prehistoric Societies*, London.

Connerton, P., 1989. *How societies remember*, Cambridge.

Dodgshon, R.A., 1998. *Society in Time and Space. A Geographical Perspective on Change*, Cambridge.

Edmonds, M., 1999. *Ancestral Geographies of the Neolithic*, London.

Fentress, J. and Wickham, C., 1992. *Social Memory*, Oxford.

Gjerde, J.M.S. 1998. *A different use of landscape? The visual landscape study of rock art styles in Hardanger, Western Norway. A method of dating?* Unpublished MA thesis, University of Reading.

Gjerde, J.M.S., 2002. 'Lokalisering av helleristninger i landskapet', *Bilder av bronsålder*, J. Goldhahn (ed.), [Acta

Archaeologica Lundensia, Series in 8° no. 37], Gothenburg, 23-51.

Halbwachs, M., 1992. *On Collective Memory*, edited, translated and with an introduction by L.A. Coser, Chicago.

Ingold, T., 2000. *The Perception of the Environment. Essays on livelihood, dwelling and skill*, London.

Kaul, F., 1998. *Ships on Bronzes. A Study in Bronze Age Religion and Iconography*, [PNM Studies in Archaeology and History 3.1/2, Copenhagen.

Larsen, G.M., 1972. *Bergbilder i Hordaland. En undersøkelse av bildenes sammensetning, deres naturmiljø og kulturmiljø*, [Årbok for Universitetet i Bergen, Humanistisk Serie 1970, no 2], Bergen.

Ling, J., 2005. 'The fluidity of rock art', *Mellan sten och järn*, J. Goldhahn (ed.), [Rapport från det 9,e nordiska bronsålderssymposiet, Gotarc Serie C, Arkeologiske skrifter No 59], Gothenburg, 437-60.

Linge, T.E., 2005. 'Kammeranlegget i Mjeltehaugen – eit rekonstruksjonsforslag', *Mellan sten och järn*, J. Goldhahn (ed.), [Rapport från det 9,e nordiska bronsålderssymposiet, Gotarc Serie C, Arkeologiske skrifter No 59], Gothenburg, 537-59.

Linge, T.E., 2007. *Mjeltehaugen, fragment frå gravritual*, [Universitetet i Bergen Arkeologiske skrifter, Hovedfag/Master 3], Bergen.

Lødøen, T.K., 2005. 'Berge i Strandebarm', *Bergkunst. Helleristninger i Noreg*, G. Mandt and T.K. Lødøen (eds.), Oslo, 194-205.

Mandt, G., 1983. 'Tradition and Diffusion in West-Norwegian Rock Art. Mjeltehaugen revisited', *Norwegian Archaeological Review* 16.1, 14-32.

Mandt, G., 1991. *Vestnorske ristninger i tid og rom* vol. I-II. Unpublished PhD thesis, University of Bergen.

Mandt, G., 2002. 'Hardanger - en mangfoldig ristningsregion', *Arkeo* 1, 9-14.

Sognnes, K., 1987. *Bergkunsten i Stjørdal 2*, [Gunneria 56], Trondheim.

Sognnes, K., 2003. 'On shoreline dating of rock art', *Acta Archaeologica* 73, 189-209.

Stewart, P.J. and Strathern, A., 2003. 'Introduction', 2003. *Landscape, Memory and History*, P.J. Stewart and A. Strathern (eds.), London and Sterling, 1-15.

Straub, J., 2002. 'Personal and Collective Identity. A Conceptual Analysis', *Identities. Time, Difference, and Boundaries*, H. Friese (ed.), New York and Oxford, 56-76.

Taçon, P., 1994. 'Socializing landscapes, the long-term implications of signs, symbols and marks on the land', *Archaeology in Oceania* 29, 117-29.

Tilley, C., 1999. *Metaphor and Material Culture*, Oxford.

Wahlgren, K.H., 2002. *Bilder av betydelse*, [Stockholm Studies in Archaeology 23], Stockholm.

Wertsch, J., 2002. *Voices of Collective Remembering*, Cambridge.

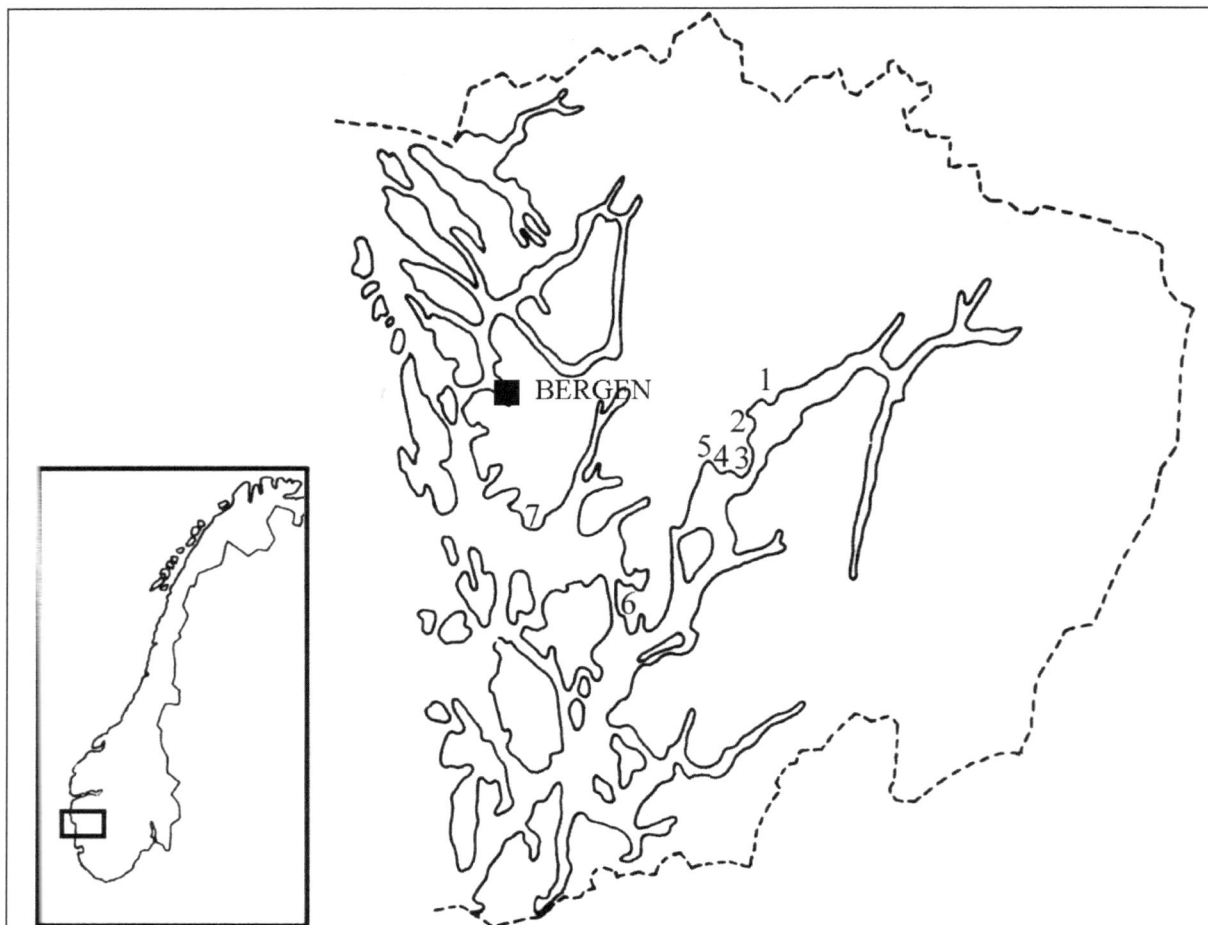

Figure 1. The Hardangerfjord area. 1=Rykkje, 2=Fonnaland, 3=Vangdal 1-2, 4=Linga, 5= Berge, 6= Hammarhaug, 7=Halhjem.

Figure 2. Rykkje

Figure 3. Vangdal. The Bronze Age carvings are located near the ground to the left, the Stone Age carvings on the top of the outcrop, in between the trees.

Figure 4. Fonnaland

Figure 5. Linga.

Figure 6. Berge

Figure 7. Hammarhaug

Figure 8. Halhjem

Living in the mountains, Arkadian identity in the classical period

James Roy

Among Greeks in classical antiquity there were several levels of communal identity, of which the highest was a sense of common Greekness. Mainland Greece was then divided into several regions, each with its own regional identity. Some regions were controlled by a single community, notable examples are Attica, controlled by Athens, and Corinthia, controlled by Corinth. It was however much commoner for a region to contain several communities that shared a common regional identity but had each its own identity. Arkadia was an example of the latter, commoner, category, and it is the topic of this paper. It was to some extent a special case because of its geographical situation in the centre of the Peloponnese, in a largely mountainous area with direct access to the sea only at Phigalia in the southwest (and in the region Triphylia, adjacent to Phigalia, while it formed part of Arkadia in the fourth and third centuries BC). One question is thus whether the common regional identity of the Arkadians was affected by their upland environment. Another consideration is the extent to which modern understanding of ancient Arkadia and its regional identity have been distorted by misleading preconceptions.

The great majority of ancient Greek communities lay on or near the sea. Their territories extended typically from the coast, or least low-lying plains, over higher land to mountain. Within them human settlement and human activity was concentrated on land at lower altitudes, though the uplands could be exploited notably as pasture but also for a variety of other purposes. Arkadia, however, apart from a few areas like Phigalia at the western edge of the area, had no low land. The valleys or basins among the mountains were at altitudes ranging from c. 450 m at Megalopolis to c. 950 m at Lousoi. The mountains themselves rose much higher, particularly in the north where the highest, Mt. Ziria (the ancient Mt. Kyllene) reaches 2374 m Arkadia was not the only such region in mainland Greece, for there were others in north-central Greece, but among such regions Arkadia lends itself to study as a test-case, since we are reasonably well-informed about it.

There have been recent studies of how Greeks perceived mountains and mountainous regions, though the relevant scholarly literature is still limited (Garnsey 1988; Jameson 1989; Buxton 1992; 1994; various authors in Olshausen and Sonnabend 1996; Quantin 2005). In some cases the study adopts the viewpoint of the typical Greek living at lower altitude. There was a tendency to see mountain-dwellers as savage and backward (Antonetti 1987) (comparable to an unfavourable view of Aegean island populations, Brun 1993), Gehrke (1996) has however pointed to the economic potential of mountainous parts of Greece, taking Akarnania as an example, and there have been other studies, notably Lloyd's (1991) comparison of farming in Samnium and Arkadia. Chaniotis (1991; 1995; 1996a; 1996b) has analysed how the Cretan uplands were exploited. It is clear that upland areas of Greece offered considerable economic resources, though these were obviously limited by the physical environment.

Analysis of ancient perceptions of Arkadian identity is sometimes coloured by modern views of ancient Arkadia. Oe such view is the conception of Arkadia as an idyllic pastoral setting. It is certainly true that a common form of exploiting upland Mediterranean landscapes was, and is, through flocks of sheep and goats, and Arkadia was famous in antiquity for its numerous flocks (Roy 1999, especially 331-2). Alongside the animal husbandry actually practised in Arkadia there eventually arose a literary convention that Arkadia was a land of nymphs and shepherds. Arkadia thus became the prime setting for pastoral poetry, an urban literary genre that used a rural setting as a device to achieve various poetic effects without seeking to offer a realistic depiction of the countryside, although it could of course incorporate some realistic detail. Virgil has been credited with establishing Arkadia as the prime pastoral setting (Snell 1945), though his role has been disputed (Jachmann 1952), and scholarly literature on Arkadia's role as an idyllic setting continues to grow (Rosenmeyer 1969; 232-46; Sakellariou 1997; D'Anna 1998; La Penna 2004; Suerbaum 2005). This literary convention was also adopted by the visual arts, the best-known example being Poussin's painting, now in the Louvre, of three shepherds and a nymph looking at a tomb set in a rural landscape and bearing the inscription 'Et in Arcadia ego'. Although a quite artificial literary device, the notion that Arkadia was a pastoral landscape seems to have led some moderns to see the historical Arkadia in those terms. Pritchett (1999, 16 n.7), for instance, although a scholar generally concerned to offer conclusions about ancient Greek topography and institutions based on carefully considered evidence, has written that 'The religion of the Arkadians was such as we might expect from a nation of shepherds and huntsmen'.

Another modern view, possibly related, is that Arkadia was a particularly poor region of Greece. Greeks living in a mountain landscape certainly had some disadvantages in comparison with Greeks elsewhere, harsh winters, for instance, limited the growing season for crops. Also, in a mountain landscape, the area of arable land was restricted. Nonetheless it should not be assumed out of hand that Arkadians were exceptionally poor. Many Arkadian valleys had good agricultural land, and there were clearly numerous flocks of sheep and goats, as well as other resources of economic value, such as wood from the forests (Forbes 1996). In these conditions the prosperity of individual Arkadians would depend on a range of factors, such as who had access to the resources, but the size of the population that the resources had to support would be of prime importance. Hodkinson and Hodkinson (1981) have shown how the agricultural land of Mantinea must have been very heavily exploited around 400 BC (for the Asea area, Forsén and Forsén 2003). It seems that in the classical period the Arkadian population was kept within (presumably) tolerable limits by the emigration of male Arkadians, very often to serve as mercenary soldiers. It should be noted however that the Arkadian mercenaries were typically hoplites, presumably drawn not from the poorest levels of society but from families sufficiently prosperous to equip and train their sons to fight as heavy infantry (Roy 2004). The economies of the Arkadian communities seem to have depended mainly on the natural resources of the landscape, and the economy could not expand beyond the limits imposed by the landscape. There was thus a limit to the population that Arkadia could support, and in that sense Arkadia was poor. It does not follow that the Arkadian population lived in significantly greater poverty than many other regions of Greece.

It is worth pointing out that a great deal of research has been done recently on ancient roads in Arkadia (as in other regions of Greece), notably by Pikoulas (1988; 1995; 1999; 2007). Because of the prevalence of different forms of rock ancient roads are preserved in eastern Arkadia much better than in the west. The evidence now available from eastern Arkadia shows a well-developed network of wagon-roads, and that shows that transport in this mountain region could move fairly freely and that Arkadia was not shut off from the rest of the Greek world.

There were numerous communities within Arkadia. Some of them formed sub-regional groupings often referred to (for want of a better term) as 'tribes', such as the Parrhasians of southwestern Arkadia. These tribes offered another layer of identity between the local community and the Arkadian regional consciousness, but the last of them disappeared in the fourth century BC when they were incorporated in Megalopolis (Nielsen 2002, 271-302). Among the local communities of Arkadia in the classical period the polis or city-state became the norm, as elsewhere in Greece (Nielsen 2002; 2004). The sense of identity within the individual polis was strong, but there was nonetheless also a clear sense of Arkadian identity. As often in Greece it was expressed through a mythical common ancestor, allowing a 'memory' of common descent. Elements of such Arkadian myth appear in surviving poetry at least from the sixth century, but the fullest surviving version of the Arkadian charter-myth is found in the work of Pausanias, writing in the second century AD (Nielsen 1999). It presents the genealogy of Arkas, ancestor of all the Arkadians. The most striking expression of Arkas' significance for Arkadians is the monument set up at Delphi by the Arkadian confederacy founded in 370 BC that briefly united all Arkadia (*CEG* 2.824, on the confederacy Roy 2000a). On it stood the statues of Arkas and his sons, the latter symbolising different parts of Arkadia. The sons on the monument included Triphylos, a son added to represent the region Triphylia to the west of Arkadia since Triphylia had very recently declared itself Arkadian. Arkadian identity was also proclaimed on the coins struck in the fifth century with the legend 'Arkadikon' (or an abbreviation of the word).

The coins also showed the head of Zeus Lykaios, whose cult, celebrated at his sanctuary on the summit of Mt. Lykaion, was greatly respected by Arkadians. These coins clearly proclaim a sense of common Arkadian identity, though it is still unclear where they were struck or why. Similar coins, with the same legend and with Zeus Lykaios, were struck by the fourth-century BC confederacy, using Arkadian identity for a clearly political purpose (there are good examples of both fifth‾ and fourth-century BC Arkadian coins in Walker 2006, for the earlier period nos. 1393-412, 1451-69, and 1709-16, and for the later nos. 1511-39).

However, political unification of ancient Arkadia was rare, and the shared sense of Arkadian identity was rarely reflected in a political structure. The sense of identity nonetheless remained strong. It is seen very clearly in – to name only two examples – the work of the Arkadian historian Polybius, writing in the second century BC, and in the description of Arkadia written in the second century AD by Pausanias after visiting the region. It was reinforced by some common patterns of behaviour. One was a strong emphasis on teaching music to the young, and on performing it later in life (Polybius 4.20.1-21.12). Oddly the favourite composers of the Arkadians in Polybius' day were Philoxenos and Timotheos who in their own time (late fifth and early fourth centuries BC) had been considered avant-garde (Wallace 2003). To judge by surviving inscriptions the same dialect, with local variations, was spoken across Arkadia (Dubois 1986), which may have had a unifying effect, but in the fourth century BC the Triphylians, whose dialect was different, were accepted as Arkadians.

It is difficult to trace specifically Arkadian patterns in the material record. The latest study of the available evidence finds variation across Arkadia rather than homogeneity (Morgan 1999). Patterns can be seen in some areas within the region. For instance, in the later archaic and early classical period several communities of southern Arkadia built impressive temples. These were erected not only by large communities but also by smaller places such as Pallantion, Asea, and Alipheira. Some of these temples show distinctive local features, being unusually long in relation to their width and having a side door (Østby 1990-1a; 1990-1b; 1992-3; Voyatzis 1999).

The Arkadians tended to project themselves as an old people. Whereas the charter-myths of many regions of Greece supposed that an ancestor or ancestors had come from elsewhere, the Arkadians were one of the few Greek regions to claim to be autochthonous (Nielsen 1999; Picaut and Brulé 1996 on autochthony generally). They therefore naturally also claimed to have occupied their territory since remote antiquity. They were, they said, older than the moon. They were also known as acorn-eaters (Tortzen 1996). Some types of acorn are perfectly edible, and there is nothing unusual about eating them (Megaloudi 2006, 63-4), but to categorise oneself as an acorn-eater is to present oneself as eating produce gathered from the wild rather than consuming the food, particularly cereals, produced by settled, civilised, agriculture. Such an image probably distanced the Arkadians from most Greeks, who were in any case not accustomed to living in a mountain environment. Opinions held about the Arkadians may have been reinforced by the belief that the Arkadians practised human sacrifice as part of the cult of Zeus Lykaios on Mt. Lykaion. No archaeological evidence of human sacrifice has so far been found on Mt. Lykaion, and some modern writers have dismissed the admittedly limited evidence for such sacrifice, but a good case has been made for accepting the ancient reports (Halm-Tisserand 1993, 127-58; Jost 2002). Pausanias visited Mt. Lykaion and makes a very guarded comment (8.38.7), 'On that altar they sacrifice to Zeus Lykaios in secret, and it did not suit me to be overly curious about matters concerning the sacrifice, let it be as it is and as it was from the beginning'.

This raises the question of whether in Pausanias' day, when Greece was under Roman rule, human sacrifice would have been tolerated, even as a secret rite, and if the sacrifice truly continued to be, as he says, as it had always been, that would throw doubt on any earlier practice of human sacrifice. Nonetheless, whether or not human sacrifice was actually carried out, some Greeks of the classical period evidently believed that it was, which would in itself have been enough to confirm a view that the Arkadians were, at least in some ways, different and more primitive than other Greeks.

A different impression of the Arkadians is given in a well-known passage of Polybius (4.16.11-21.12), himself an Arkadian from Megalopolis. In it Polybius is concerned to explain how the people of Kynaitha in northern Arkadia brought upon themselves by their immoral behaviour, as he saw it, a political and social disaster in which many died. The Arkadians, he argued, maintained high moral standards in a harsh environment by observing Arkadian traditions, and above all training and practice in music, but the Kynaithans failed to follow those traditions and so, exceptionally among Arkadians, fell into immorality and paid the price. Polybius, unsurprisingly, stresses the high moral standards of his fellow-Arkadians, and, although he admits that their homeland is a harsh environment that could in his view have a deleterious effect on its inhabitants, he insists that the Arkadians could, and did, overcome the harshness of their environment by proper standards of behaviour. Interestingly he does not suggest that the environment was poor or that it might lead men to immorality because of poverty.

These various perceptions of the Arkadians did not seek to take account of all that Arkadians actually did. To anyone who argued that they were backward or primitive it could have been replied that the grand temples built in southern Arkadia in the later archaic and early classical periods were built by men aware of the latest architectural achievements elsewhere in Greece; that the coins struck in Arkadia in the fifth and fourth centuries BC included some very fine examples of current Greek styles of coin-engraving; that the new Arkadian city Megalopolis founded c. 370 BC included some notable buildings and was one of the first Greek cities with a circular orchestra (Roy 2007, 294); that the numerous wagon-roads of which traces survive in eastern Arkadia show that, despite the mountains, there were regular routes for transport into and across Arkadia; and so on. It is not difficult to build an argument that Arkadia, at least from the sixth century onwards, was in touch with the main trends in Greek society and ready to follow them. But perceptions of Arkadian identity were not built on any such reckoning.

One final consideration is our own difficulty in deciding exactly how far Arkadian identity extended. Arkadia certainly expanded and contracted over time, the addition of Triphylia in the fourth century BC and its subsequent loss offer a prime example. It is therefore not surprising that it is sometimes difficult to tell how Arkadian a community at the edge of Arkadia actually was. A century ago Kourouniotis (1902) excavated a religious sanctuary on the south slope of Mt. Lykaion above the modern village Berekla (now officially Neda). The site was identified from inscriptions found at the site as a sanctuary of the god Pan. It is otherwise unknown, and does not appear to have been visited by Pausanias during his extensive tour of Arkadia. Its situation does not match what Pausanias (8.38.11) says of a sanctuary of Pan on the Nomian mountains (which he also apparently did not visit), and when describing his route from Lykosoura on the eastern slopes of Mt. Lykaion to Phigalia

southwest of Lykaion (8.39.1) he makes no mention of a sanctuary of Pan, probably because he went through northern Messenia, well south of Berekla (Jost 1985, 178-9, 187, 467-8; 1998, 258). It is not known to which city-state the sanctuary belonged; Megalopolis held the summit of Mt. Lykaion and its eastern slope, while the famous sanctuary of Apollo at Bassai, some kilometres to the west of the site, belonged to Phigalia. The excavations at Berekla produced figurines similar to those found at the sanctuary of Zeus on the summit of Mt. Lykaion and those found at Lykosoura on the eastern slope of Mt. Lykaion, both of these sites being Arkadian (Lamb 1925-6; Jost 1975; Felten 1988; Hübinger 1992; 1993). The sanctuary lies just north of the upper waters of the River Neda, normally considered to be the boundary between Arkadia and Messenia. For these reasons the site is today generally considered Arkadian, but it is impossible to tell whether the sanctuary was also frequented by Messenians. A figurine of Hermes on display in the National Museum in Athens was said by the man who sold it to the Archaiologike Etaireia in the 19th century to have come from Mt. Ithome, and it strongly resembles the figurines of Berekla (inventory number 7539, see Fuchs and Floren 1987, 226 n.106; I am grateful to Dr. E. Kourinou for this information). Whether this figurine is taken as evidence that a worshipper at Berekla subsequently visited Ithome, or as evidence that one of the bronzesmiths who produced the distinctive figurines of Berekla, Mt. Lykaion, and Lykosoura also worked at Ithome, it suggests Messenian connections at Berekla. Arkadian identity was not sharply delimited, nor neatly separated from Arkadia's neighbours (Roy 2000b).

References

Antonetti, C., 1987. 'Agraioi et agrioi. Montagnards et bergers; un prototype diachronique de sauvagerie', *Dialogues d'Histoire Ancienne* 13, 199-236.

Brun, P., 1993. 'La faiblesse insulaire , histoire d'un topos', *Zeitschrift für Papyrologie und Epigraphik* 99, 165-83.

Buxton, R., 1992. 'Imaginary Greek mountains', *Journal of Hellenic Studies* 112, 1-15.

Buxton, R., 1994. *Imaginary Greece. The contexts of mythology*, Cambridge.

Chaniotis, A., 1991. 'Von Hirten, Kräutersammlern, Epheben, und Pilgern, Leben auf den Bergen im antiken Kreta', *Ktéma* 16, 93-109 [also published as Chaniotis 1996b].

Chaniotis, A., 1995. 'Problems of 'pastoralism' and 'transhumance' in classical and Hellenistic Crete', *Orbis Terrarum* 1, 1-51.

Chaniotis, A., 1996a. 'Die kretischen Berge als Wirtschaftsraum', *Stuttgarter Kolloquium zur historischen Geographie des Altertums 5, 1993, Gebirgsland als Lebensraum*, E. Olshausen and H. Sonnabend (eds.), [Geographica historica 8], Amsterdam, 255-66.

Chaniotis, A., 1996b. 'Von Hirten, Kräutersammlern, Epheben und Pilgern, Leben auf den Bergen im antiken Kreta', *Nature et paysage dans la pensée et l'environnement des civilisations antiques*, G. Siebert (ed.), [Université des Sciences Humaines de Strasbourg, Travaux du Centre du Recherche sur le Proche-orient et la Grèce Antiques 14], Paris, 91-107, [also published as Chaniotis 1991].

D'Anna, G., 1998. 'La natura idealizzata, l'Arcadia nella poesia classica', *L'uomo antico e la natura, Torino 28-29-30 aprile 1997*, R. Uglione (ed.), Turin, 251-69.

Dubois, L., 1986. *Recherches sur le dialecte arcadien* (3 vols. in one), Louvain-la-Neuve.

Felten, F., 1988. 'Archaische Arkadische Bronzestatuetten', *Griechische und römische Statuetten und Grossbronzen. Akten der 9. Internationalen Tagung über antike Bronzen*, K. Gschwantler and A. Bernhard-Walcher (eds.), Vienna, 237-43.

Forbes, H., 1996. 'The uses of the uncultivated landscape in modern Greece, a pointer to the value of the wilderness', *Human landscapes in classical antiquity, environment and culture*, G. Shipley and J. Salmon (eds.), London and New York, 68-97.

Forsén, J. and Forsén B., 2003. *The Asea Valley Survey. An Arcadian mountain valley from the Palaeolithic period until Modern times*, Stockholm.

Fuchs, V., and Floren, J., 1987. *Die griechische Plastik* Band I, Munich.

Garnsey, P., 1988. 'Mountain economies in southern Europe. Thoughts on the early history, continuity and individuality of Mediterranean upland pastoralism', *Pastoral economies in classical antiquity*, C. R. Whittaker (ed.), [Cambridge Philological Society Supplementary 14], Cambridge, 177-209.

Gehrke, H.-J., 1996. 'Bergland als Wirtschaftsraum. Das Beispiel Akarnaniens', *Stuttgarter Kolloquium zur historischen Geographie des Altertums 5, 1993, Gebirgsland als Lebensraum. E. Olshausen and H. Sonnabend (eds.), [Geographica historica 8], Amsterdam, 71-7.

Halm-Tisserant, M., 1993. *Cannibalisme et immortalité, l'enfant dans le chaudron en Grèce ancienne*, Paris.

Hodkinson, S., and Hodkinson, H., 1981. 'Mantineia and the Mantinike, settlement and society in a Greek polis', *Annual of the British School at Athens* 76, 239-96.

Hübinger, U., 1992. 'On Pan's iconography and the cult in the *Sanctuary of Pan* on the slopes of Mount Lykaon', *The iconography of Greek cult in the archaic and classical periods*, R. Hägg (ed.), [*Kernos* Supplément 1], Athens and Liège, 189-212.

Hübinger, U., 1993. 'Überlegungen zu den Bronzestatuetten aus dem 'Pan'-Heiligtum am Südabhang des Lykaion', *Sculpture from Arcadia and Laconia*, O. Palagia and W. Coulson (eds.), Oxford, 25-31.

Jachmann, G., 1952. 'L'Arcadia come paesaggio bucolico', *Maia* 5, 161-74.

Jameson, M.H., 1989. 'Mountains and the Greek city-states', *Montagnes, fleuves, forêts dans l'histoire, barrières ou lignes de convergence? (= Berge, Flüsse, Wälder in der Geschichte, Hindernisse oder Begegnungsräume?)*, J.-F. Bergier (ed.), [Travaux présentés au XVIe Congrès International des Sciences Historiques, Stuttgart, août 1985], St. Katharinen, 7-17.

Jost, M., 1975. 'Statuettes de bronze archaïques provenant de Lykosoura', *Bulletin de Correspondance Hellénique* 99, 339-64.

Jost, M., 1985. *Sanctuaires et cultes d'Arcadie*, [École Française d'Athènes, Études Péloponnésiennes 9], Paris.

Jost, M., 2002. 'À propos des sacrifices humains dans le sanctuaire de Zeus du mont Lycée', *Peloponnesian sanctuaries and cults*, R. Hägg (ed.), [Acta Instituti Atheniensis Regni Sueciae, Series 4°, 48], Stockholm, 183-6.

Jost, M., 1998. 'Commentary in M. Casevitz, M. Jost and J. Marcadé', *Pausanias, Description de la Grèc,* Livre VIII, *L'Arcadie*, Paris.

Kourouniotis, K., 1902. 'Ἀνασκαφή ιερού Νομίου Πανός', *Πρακτικά*, 72-5.

La Penna, A., 2004. 'Fasto e povertà nell'*Eneide*', *Maia* 56, 225-48.

Lamb, W., 1925-6. 'Arcadian bronze statuettes', *Annual of the British School at Athens* 27, 133-48.

Lloyd, J., 1991. 'Farming the highlands, Samnium and Arcadia in the Hellenistic and early Roman imperial periods', *Roman landscapes. Archaeological survey in the Mediterranean region*, G. Barker and J.A. Lloyd (eds.), [Archaeological Monographs of the British School at Rome 2], London, 180-93.

Megaloudi, F., 2006. *Plants and diet in Greece from Neolithic to Classic Periods. The archaeobotanical remains*, [BAR International Series 1516], Oxford.

Morgan, C., 1999. 'Cultural subzones in early Iron Age and Archaic Arkadia', *Defining ancient Arkadia*, T.H. Nielsen and J. Roy (eds.), [Acts of the Copenhagen Polis Centre 6], Copenhagen, 382-456.

Nielsen, T.H., 1999. 'The concept of Arkadia – the people, their land, and their organisation', *Defining ancient Arkadia*, T.H. Nielsen and J. Roy (eds.), [Acts of the Copenhagen Polis Centre 6], Copenhagen, 16-79.

Nielsen, T.H., 2002. *Arkadia and its poleis in the archaic and classical periods*, [Hypomnemata 140], Göttingen.

Nielsen, T.H., 2004. 'Arkadia', *An inventory of archaic and classical Greek poleis*, M. H. Hansen, and T. H. Nielsen (eds.), Oxford, 505-39.

Olshausen, E., and Sonnabend, H. (eds.), 1996. *Stuttgarter Kolloquium zur historischen Geographie des Altertums 5, 1993, Gebirgsland als Lebensraum*, [Geographica historica 8], Amsterdam.

Østby, E., 1990-1a. 'I templi di Pallantion', *Arnuario della Scuola Archeologica di Atene* 68-9, 53-93

Østby, E., 1990-1b. 'Templi di Pallantion e dell'Arcadia, confronti e sviluppi', *Annuario della Scuola Archeologica di Atene* 68-9, 285-391.

Østby, E., 1992-3. 'The temples of Pallantion and archaic temple architecture of Arcadia', *Peloponnesiaka* Supplement 19 (*Ποακτικά του Δ' Διεθνούς Συνεδρίου Πελοποννησιακών Σπουδών*) Vol. 2, 65-75.

Picaut, J.-F., and Brulé, P. (eds.), 1996. *Poikilia 1996*, Rennes, Université de Rennes 2.

Pikoulas, Y. A., 1988. *Η νότια Μεγαλοπολιτική χώρα από τον 4° π.Χ. ως τον 8° τ.Χ. αιώνα*, [Ηορος], Athens.

Pikoulas, Y. A., 1995. Οδικό δίκτυο και Άμυνα από την Κόρινθο στο Άργος και την Αρκαδία, [Ηορος], Athens.

Pikoulas, Y., 1999. 'The road-network of Arkadia', *Defining ancient Arkadia*, T.H. Nielsen and J. Roy (eds.), [Acts of the Copenhagen Polis Centre 6], Copenhagen, 248-319.

Pikoulas, Y., 2007. 'Travelling by land in ancient Greece', *Travel, geography and culture in ancient Greece and the Near East*, C. Adams and J. Roy (eds.), Oxford, 78-87.

Pritchett, W. K., 1999. *Pausanias Periegetes* Vol. 2, Amsterdam, Gieben.

Quantin, F., 2005. 'A propos de l'imaginaire montagnard en Grèce ancienne', *Montagnes sacrées d'Europe*, S. Brunet, D. Julia, and N. Lemaire (eds.), Paris, 23-34.

Rosenmeyer, T. G., 1969. *The green cabinet, Theocritus and the European pastoral lyric*, Berkeley and Los Angeles.

Roy, J., 1999. 'The economies of Arkadia', *Defining ancient Arkadia*, T.H. Nielsen and J. Roy (eds.), [Acts of the Copenhagen Polis Centre 6], Copenhagen, 320-81.

Roy, J., 2000a. 'Problems of democracy in the Arcadian confederacy 370-62 BC', *Alternatives to Athens, varieties of political organization and community in ancient Greece*, R.W. Brock and S.J. Hodkinson (eds.), Oxford, 308-26.

Roy, J., 2000b. 'The frontier between Arkadia and Elis in classical antiquity', *Polis and politics, studies in ancient Greek history presented to Mogens Herman Hansen on his sixtieth birthday, August 20th, 2000*, P. Flensted-Jensen, T.H. Nielsen and L. Rubinstein (eds.), Copenhagen, 133-56.

Roy, J., 2004. 'The ambitions of a mercenary', *The long march*, R. Lane Fox (ed.), New Haven and London, 264-88.

Roy, J., 2007. 'The urban layout of Megalopolis in its civic and confederate context', *Building Communities, house, settlement and society in the Aegean and beyond*, R. Westgate, N. Fisher, and J. Whitley (eds.), [British School at Athens Studies 15], London, 289-95.

Sakellariou, A. I., 1996-7. 'Ο βουκολικός Βεργίλιος και η Αρκαδία,' *Peloponnesiaka* 22, 351-8.

Snell, B., 1945. 'Arkadien, die Entdeckung einer geistigen Landschaft', *Antike und Abendland* 1, 26-41.

Suerbaum, W., 2005. 'Von Arkadien nach Rom. Bukolisches in der *Aeneis* Vergils', *Philologus* 149, 278-96.

Tortzen, C. G., 1996. 'Agernspisende mænd i Arkadien findes i mængde', *Hvad tales her om? Festskrift til Johnny Christensen*, M.S. Christensen, S. Ebbesen, M.H. Hansen, J. Mejer, T. H. Nielsen, C. G. Tortzen (eds.), Copenhagen, 127-37.

Voyatzis, M. E., 1999. 'The role of temple-building in consolidating Arkadian communities.' *Defining ancient Arkadia*, T.H. Nielsen and J. Roy (eds.), [Acts of the Copenhagen Polis Centre 6], Copenhagen, 130-68.

Walker, A., 2006. *Coins of the Peloponnesos, the BCD Collection (Auktion LHS 96)*, Zürich.

Wallace, R. W., 2003. 'An early fifth-century Athenian revolution in aulos music', *Harvard Studies in Classical Philology* 101, 73-92.

The Formation of Female Identity in Ancient Sparta through Kinetics

Pandelis Constantinakos and Metaxia Papapostolou

We will start our paper by quoting Aristotle (*Politica* 1337a) when he says: 'No one can deny the fact that it is the duty of a legislator to provide for the education of the young because in any city-state, that it is not done, the constitution is breached... Since the enhancement and education of every citizen must abide by its constitution...Since the final purpose of the city-state is one and the same. It is obvious that the purpose must be one and common for all. The provisions and structure of any learning-education system, therefore should be the responsibility of the community (of the commune) and not of a personal nature as it exists today where each individual cares for his children's teaching, teaching them what 'each one of us' believes is best. That is why what has to do with the community must be taught by the whole community. For this to happen, each citizen must believe he belongs to a 'whole', that he is 'a small part of this whole'. And thus provision for each member or each part means provision for 'the whole'' (*Politica* 1337α).

It is to this fact that the 'Lacedaemonians' are attributed for, this attribute of being part of a whole for the well-being of 'the whole' which is greatly instilled throughout their life. In order for this attribute to be enhanced the young, both boys and girls sustain the same learning-education throughout their life.

Sparta was the only city-state to impose a 'common' inter-dependence among the fields of education, politics, economy and social activities. The educational system was mandatory, co-educational and the same both for boys and girls. The sense of 'Emeis'-'We' rather than the 'Ego'-'I' was greatly imposed (Ιστορία των Ελλήνων 1971, 518). Thus the young individual learnt to identify himself with regard to the whole rather than to his 'individuality' (Birgalias 1999; Ducat 2006; Kennell 1995). This essence, 'of commonness' of 'being part of something' strongly pre-dominated in every part or activity of daily life. From the beginning pf the 6th century BC till the 5th century BC. Then in every city-state each 'individual-citizen' was governed by the state and his existence was, inter-dependent on it. The individual was a reflection of society and existed and acted in accordance with the rules of society. The essence of each individual was his co-existence of 'him' with 'the others'. This was strongly reinforced and rewarded, so that the individual believed that without this kind of existence his life was non-existents (Ιστορία των Ελλήνων 1971, 518).

The novelty of this educational system of the Spartans is how their education is closely-knitted with the social, political and economic aspects of society. The idea of 'togetherness' or 'wholeness' is focused and imposed in their conduct. Lastly, it can be noted that the state takes complete responsibility for educating its citizens through a 'public means' which is 'the same' and 'mandatory' for all. In this way the state is ensured that certain attributes are instilled to create a true-Spartan-citizen. It is for the benefit of the whole society that this system must be abided by, regardless of the race or gender. A young person's attributes are not dependent on his blood-relatives and cannot be passed down. In contrast, they have to be acquired and won and, for those who know how best to contribute to the success and, implementation of this, they are rewarded and distinguished.

People in other states considered the Spartan way of life and learning as the reason for its fame and success in every aspect of their society. Well-known personalities, such as the philosopher Platon, the historian Xenophon and the orator Socrates all acknowledged the fact that it was the way Spartans trained their young (physically, socially, politically and morally) that was the basis for their success and victories. Moreover, they believed that this system could be adopted by other city-state.

The main focus of this system relied on the strenuous-rigorous exercise and of the body to tolerate the cold, the heat, hunger, thirst and pain (Baltrusch 2004, 72-5; Cartledge 2004, 40-1; Ducat 2006, 245).

It required that the young learn to be obedient above all. Any attribute which was acquired had to be favorable to all its members the girls were trained and educated in their two basic roles as good mothers and housekeepers. This meant that they were required to learn how to supervise staff, maintain household duties and keep accounts. Spartan women are to have been able to maintain two households at the same time. As expected, the boys were trained for war (Baltrusch 2004, 72-5).

Apart from the value of social-equality which predominated, other values were acquired, such as the value of obeying rules, at any cost, and the value of honor and glory. Most important of all, is that both men and women gained equal opportunities to education and

were encouraged to value competence and excellence, thus they strove to surpass and to excel. Young men and women competed for honorable positions in the state. Their social-status was not hereditary but acquired and gained through competence and competition. Men and women existed in a complementary relationship. This phenomenon was quite unusual at that time since we have documentation of many contemporaries expressing 'disdai' and ridicule of this system (Pomeroy 2002, 7-8).

At this point we must emphasize that in order for this equality to exist girls from birth were brought up in the same way as boys. This is certainly unique and it has been brought to the attention to historians like Xenophon and Plutarch who sought to find the reasons behind this way of upbringing. Xenophon (*Lacedaemonians Politeia* 1.4) writes: 'And that is why first of all Lycurgus ordered girls to train like boys, then he ordered that women compete among themselves just like men, in running, in strength and in stamina; Lycurgus believed that when both men and women were strong, their children would be stronger'. The girls' bodies were built from their participation in events like: running, wrestling, throwing the javelin, throwing the accordion (Plutarch, *Lycurgus* 14.2-3; *Ethica* 227 D). Mothers had to be strong so that their babies would be just as strong. Women were also required to compete in official athletic events which had been introduced in Sparta and they also took part in religious ceremonies. This way of training brought about Pan-hellenic fame, prestige and glamour (Doukas 1922, 85-6; Kargakos 2006, 538-40; Kyle 2007, 184-5; Pappas 2007, 388).

Evidence of the above is seen in Plutarch work where he refers to the girls' strenuous exercise, equal to that of boys so that eventually girls could acquire strong bodies to bear strong babies. He continues to say that young Spartan women were not restrained in their homes, some thing common in other states, but were brought up like boys. They trained and complete outdoors, in public so that their graces and abilities and competences could be displayed (Birgalias 1999, 256; Cartledge 2004, 238-9; Ducat 2006, 232-7; Hodkinson 2001, 300-26).

Other instances of women's public display are the well-known dances, named 'the Parthenia' by 'Ale manes'. Women danced and sang and displayed their attributes in public so that they could be distinguished and rewarded. People could actually see and distinguished the special attributes of the women who danced and sang in these well-known dances (Arrigoni 2007, 72; Flaceliere 2005, 109).

Plutarch goes on to say: 'That this form, of upbringing made women strong and combated weakness. It prepared women to endure the pains of labor and successfully prepared them for more 'harmonic marriages' due to their compatility to men'. He adds: 'The nudity of the girls was in no way 'immorally provoking' or 'ostentatious'; rather, it emitted feeling of 'shyness' and 'timidity' (Plutarch, *Lycurgus* 14.2-3). In this way the girls learnt to be as simple and as healthy as possible demanding to be regarded as 'equals' since they believed that they did not lack in any of the men's virtues' (Baltrusch 2004, 87-94).

Other sources, like Propetrios (3-14, 1-20), shows us that women took part in athletic events like the 'Pagrateion', boxing, hunting and even in war. They participated in athletic competitions at the ancient temple of Artemis at Vravrona and at the ceremony which honored Hera at Olympia (Hodkinson 2001, 300-26). Although we know that women were not allowed to take part in the Olympic Games we cannot be sure how women in Sparta met these restriction. What we do know is that about 400 BC a young Spartan woman named Kyniska, King Archidamos' daughter was crowed as an Olympic winner in chariot racing. According to the rules the winner of chariot racing was not the chariot

winner. but the owner of the horses and she is said to have been a good breeder of horses (Baltrusch 2004, 87-94, Decker 2004, 164; Kargakos 2006, 548).

Even though women participated in athletic competitions and activities, they also took part in group activities, in public places, outdoors (not home) in view of the public. Their strengths and virtues could be seen, distinguished and rewarded. They could be identified for their competence not according to background or family status but for what they actually were (Hodkinson 2001, 300-26). And all this was part of their upbringing. Moreover, the Spartan women's involvement in athletic activities definitely gave them a sense of beauty and grace as is seen in the bronze statuette dated 500 BC which represents a Spartan woman athlete running (the British Museum of London). The picture is indicative of the sense of freedom and well-being that Spartan women possessed because of their training and upbringing. The statuette reminds us of an Amazon in a short sleeveless tunic, quite unusual for archaic women, who as rule, dressed in full dresses covering the entire body.

Cosmetics evidently were not used since they were not necessary. They training outdoors made their skin shine in 'their glimmering faces' (Fantham 2004). They were referred to by their names and honored for their 'graces'. Many metaphors relating them to the animal kingdom have been used. Two of these metaphors reflect the characteristics of strength wild beauty and wealth; 'The most honorable of them stands out like a chariot horse from a common grazing one....robust, vibrant and victorious'; 'That any girl who competes with Agado in beauty is like a horse from Kalexeos competing against a horse from Ivino' (Fantham 2004). The metaphors used horses to reflect the characteristics of superiority and excellence.

Thus, this form of upbringing of rigorous physical training equipped them with a high sense of 'duty' and 'consciousness'. These characteristics favorable determined their success in life, marriage and family. The attention given to Spartan women as in no other city-state made her a 'Despoina' which as brought out from stories and anecdotes received the respect and attention of society. Moreover, it promoted their dominant role in society (Baltrusch 2004, 87-94). In no other state had women been so involved in public activities. Even though women were not part of the political structure of the state, they could take part in the decision-making of serious matters since they had freedom of speech and could influence the final decision. The 'image' or 'icon' which one visualizes of Spartan women is one of 'truly virtuous' and infinitely content. The term 'Efpsihos' is the name that will be given to the one who can overcome the first instinctive feelings of self-preservation, which in turn brings about the feeling of fear. Whoever is strong enough to overcome these two basic feelings can honestly one become truly virtuous. A virtuous person is one who complies with a basic code of ethics, who excels and stands out from period to period and from place to place. Based on these two premises Spartan women were considered 'Efpsihes' in the ancient world and among themselves (Karzis 1997, 150-5).

There are stories that talk about Spartan women who killed their own sons because they behaved cowardly before the enemy. Other stories are related to scenes of mothers running to the battle held searching for their sons' bodies only to count the wounds sustained so their sons be honoured or dishonoured. According to Karzis 1997, 150-5) there were two choices: '...One was to lead and march proudly in the procession back from war' or 'hide in their homes in shame and dishonoured'.

What must be clearly emphasized is that the austere military structure of society depended highly on Spartan women whose duty was to contribute and strengthen it. It was the mothers' duty to instill the sense of duty and honor in their sons and this could only be done, only if they had sustained the same austere military training. The mother's last words to her son off battle were: 'Ei tan ei epi tas' (Ιστορία των Ελλήνων 1971, 517-521), which means to return alive but with honour otherwise not to return at all. This strength of heart and character is also seen in King Leonida's wife Gorgos who has allegedly said that he who does his duty has every right to boast about it.

It is fact that Spartan women were known for being 'Efpsihes' and for being beautiful, refreshing and well-built. There was certainly great admiration for them and we can see this from Aristophanes' work *Lysistrate* in his using Athenian women to admire and talk about the true wild beauty of queen Labito from Sparta (Karzis 1997, 150-5).

In conclusion, the intricately-knitted pattern of Spartan society greatly played a role in the formation the women's social identity in society. Their education, their dancing, their religious ceremonies, their household duties, their responsibilities, all contributed in shaping their roles in society as equal members.

References

Arrigoni, G. 2007. *Οι Γυναίκες στην Αρχαία Ελλάδα*, (transl), Thessaloniki.

Baltrusch, E. 2004. *Σπάρτη*, (transl), Athens.

Birgalias, N. 1999. *L'odyssee de l'education Spartiate*, [Historical Monographs 20], Athens.

Cartledge, P. 2004. *Οι Σπαρτιάτες*, (transl), Athens

Decker, W. 2004. *Ο Αθλητισμός στην Ελληνική Αρχαιότητα*, (transl), Athens.

Doukas, P. 1992. Η Σπάρτη διαμέσου των αιώνων, New York.

Ducat, J. 2006. *Spartan Education*, Wales.

Fantham, E. 2004. *Οι Γυναίκες στον Αρχαίο Κόσμο*, (transl), Athens.

Faceliere, R. 2005. *Ο Δημόσιος και Ιδιωτικός Βίος των Αρχαίων Ελλήνων*, (transl), Athens.

Hodkinson, S. 2001. *Ιδιοκτησία και Πλούτος στην Κλασική Σπάρτη*, (transl), Athens.

Ιστορία των Ελλήνων 1971, *Αρχαϊκοί Χρόνοι*, τόμος $2^{ος}$, Athens.

Kargakos, S. 2006. *Ιστορία της Αρχαίας Σπάρτης Α*, Athens.

Karzis, T. 1997. *Οι Γυναίκες στα Αρχαία Χρόνια*, Athens.

Kennell, N. 1995. *The Gymnasium of Virtue*, North Carolina.

Kyle, D. 2007. *Sport and Spectacle in the Ancient World*, London.

Pappas, T. 2007. *Προσεγγίσεις στην Αρχαία Ελληνική Παιδεία*, Athens.

Pomeroy, S.B. 2002. *Spartan Women*, New York.

Memories, practice and identity. A case of early medieval migration

Magdalena Naum

Introduction

The paper is exploring a role of memory in the formation of cultural identity in the circumstances of migration. In particular, the attention is directed towards ritual practices and the role of such collective actions for reinforcing the ontological questions about selfhood, belonging to a group and identity of the immigrants. It will be put forward that the proper conduct of funerary practices served not only as a means of defining, controlling and domesticating death of a community member but participation in the rituals had a powerful socializing and bonding outcome for the mourners. For immigrants these collective memories and sharing of common knowledge rooted in cultural memory and the past might have worked as a solidification factor strengthening their feeling of identity.

The paper is also aiming at examining the effect of migration on funerary practices and efforts and solutions developed by the immigrants to communicate their otherness and cultural identity. Theoretical approaches to collective memory and collective practice are combined and exemplified by a case study of funerary rituals of early medieval Slavic immigrants on the Danish island of Bornholm.

Identities as situational constructs

There is an irrefutable link between construction of identity, migration and memory. Identities are often constructed in the situation of culture contacts, like migrations, and recognition and concretion of sameness (which grounds identification) is based on the shared collective and cultural memory. Cultural or ethnic identity is formed through group or individual self-definition while standing vis-à-vis the others. It is embedded in a specific cultural and social context and it exists as long as there are individuals who include themselves into this group. It is believed that the nature of a group is dynamic and fluid, depending on the maintenance of the boundary between members and outsiders and not on the stability in the cultural contents it encloses (Barth 1969, 14; Olsen and Kobyliński 1991, 12). This emphasis on emergence of cultural identity as an aspect and result of social relations involving culturally different others, naturally directs focus towards migration, as one of the circumstances that trigger perception and negotiation of difference. In the process of translocation immigrants do not negotiate a shift from one set of cultural identities to another but instead 'move from a world in which identity was not a central concern to one in which they are pressed with increasing force to adopt understanding of personhood and collectivity' (Rouse 1995, 370). The same might be true for the host groups that form their identity against the newcomers. Thus the situation of migration (and any other culture contact) leads to the forms of self-reflective cultural comparisons and recognition of similarity and difference in knowledge, norms, values and practices. It is in such context that particular cultural practices and beliefs become objectified and rationalized in the representation of ethnic/cultural difference.

Practice and material expressions of difference (alike the strategies and decisions of inclusion or exclusion from a group) are not fixed and undergo constant redefinition and refinement. Therefore the construction of ethnic/cultural identity, and the objectification of cultural difference that this entails, should be seen as a result of the intersection of individuals' and groups' practical knowledge with the realities of social conditions of a given historical situation (Jones 1997).

Although identity is a psychological formation embedded in self-definition there is a number of cultural elements and symbols, which, in the opinion of a group, distinguish it from other groups. And despite the fact that similarities in practice do not guarantee sensation of belonging to a group, and differences in habits do not exclude identification (Yelvington 1991, 168), the inclusion or exclusion from a group is often related to sensed similarities and divergences in tacit knowledge of the individuals and shared cultural memory.

Cultural memory

Formation of identities is explicitly related to certain modes of memory. As put by Olick and Robbins, 'Memory is a central if not the central, medium through which identities are constituted' (Olick and Robbins 1998, 133). In the present paper I use concept of cultural memory, introduced by Assmann (1995; 2006), Egyptologist and culture theoretician. Cultural memory is much different that autobiographic memory (i.e. personal memories of events and experiences) or collected memories (i.e. the aggregated individual memories of members of a group). Instead it is a concept for all knowledge that

grounds and directs behavior and experience in the interactive framework of a society and is acquired through generations in repeated societal practice and indoctrination (Assmann 1995, 125-6). It is past in the present. It comprises the body of reusable stories, 'texts, images and rituals specific to each society in each epoch, whose 'cultivation serves to stabilize and convey that society's self-image' (Assmann 1995, 132) and transmits the meanings from the past. As such cultural memory is a source of feeling of relatedness, generating sense of unity, homogeneity and consistency.

In many ways process of acquiring cultural memory (and other modes of memory) is similar or even identical with acquisition of *habitus*. The process of 'mnemonic socialization', to use Zerubavel's term, i.e. the process of learning to interpret own experiences, starts within the family, which is the first 'thought community'. This process, however, does not stop there and it continues beyond the family, as an individual enters other 'thought communities of mnemonic others' as a result of marriage, conversion to another religion or migration. This entails reinterpretation of personal recollections in light of a new mnemonic tradition (Zerubavel 1996, 286). Remembering and forgetting is thus a social phenomenon. It is always done by individuals within a context of a group these individuals belong to, hence 'there is no individual memory without social experience nor is there any collective memory without individuals participating in communal life' (Olick 1999, 346). Accenting collective aspect of memory and its intertwinement with constructing identities on one hand and its subjective character (memory is reconstructive interpretation of the past) on the other hand has a vital meaning for understanding how identities are produced, how they persist and how they change in the context of migration. It helps also to support the argument that construction of identities is a dynamic process.

Cultural memory is neither static nor objective, much of what is remembered is actually filtered and therefore inevitably distorted through a process of interpretation that usually takes place within particular social settings (Lambek and Antze 1996, xvii; Zerubavel 1996, 285; Assmann 2006, 123-4). As pointed by Assmann (1995, 130) although cultural memory relates to certain knowledge, nonetheless every contemporary context relates to this knowledge differently, 'sometimes by criticism, sometimes by preservation or by transformation'. Thus the past in the present is not about a sheer persistence of the subject matter but a question of appropriation and transfer. Consequently the images of self and a group built upon memories and recollections are likely to be mobile and permeable. Both identity and memory are then ongoing processes and not possessions or properties.

Change and persistence in cultural memory depends partly on how the cultural knowledge is constituted and partly on the social and cultural circumstances underlying transmission of knowledge. Cultivation of memory depends largely on its transmission from generation to generation and joint engagement and enactment. The shared symbols and figures of collective memory are only real insofar as individuals as members of a group regard them as such, embody them and employ them in practice (Olick 1999, 338). Cultural memory relies on specialized practice and establishment of authoritative forms of knowledge. These practices and knowledge are conveyed from experts or elderly to the other members of the group. However, as the new generations define themselves against their elders, they also bear a different relation to the past than previous generations. These generational anxieties might be even stronger in the situation of migration when subsequent generations of immigrants may be considerably aware of parallel set of norms and practices. Furthermore, depending on the level of cohesion of the immigrant group and its strategies, tensions between early mnemonic socialization and the experiences and knowledge gained after migration as a result of socialization with the 'mnemonic others' may lead to changes in practice and shifts in self-description. As pointed out by Zerubavel (1996, 290), 'being social presupposes the ability to experience events that happened to groups and communities… long before we joined them as if they were part of our own past'. Such tensions, and the feeling of being caught in between the two different traditions and cultural patterns, strengthened by the shared experience of being immigrant (or its offspring) might be also a feasible ground for construction of identity.

Ritual practice

The abrupt or gradual changes in immigrant practices are a natural outcome of migration, partially due to new realities and new social circumstances that immigrants will find themselves inserted in. Nonetheless, not all practices and collective memories will change in the same direction and in the same pace. Once reformulated after arrival some practices may shift with every generation, yet the other may be kept relatively unchanged. Whether particular past and cultural knowledge will persist or not might depend on how this knowledge is constituted and what kind of logics it is built upon. Mythic logics produce taboos and duties, knowledge consisting of immobile ancestral traditions, which should be merely repeated and in order to change require bold acts of transgression. Rational logics produce prohibitions and requirements including knowledge concerning day-to-day practical matters and can be changed through arguments and refutation (Bloch 1996, 227; Olick and Robbins 1998, 130). The kinds of practice that operates through mythic logics are rituals, particularly rites of passage. Produced and reproduced repetitively and routinely they are backbone of cultural memory, 'islands of completely different temporality suspended from time' (Assmann

1995, 129). Participation and joint experience of rituals teaches those who participate who they are, grounding a sense of belonging and reinforcing feeling of identity. 'The redundancy of ritual goes beyond verbal expression, reinforcing emotional response, and allowing participants to identify with one another in sharing an explicit sense of purpose' (De Vos and Romanussi-Ross 1995, 358). Rituals, especially rites of passage are potent for concretion of identity for one another reason. Situations requiring ritual response lead to co-presence of the members of a group creating unity by generating within each individual emotions and experiences that support, perpetuate and validate the collective consciousness. Individuals become synchronize with collective. Shared participation in ritual leads to 'collective effervescence'; the particularity of situation that requires ritual response brings individuals together. These individuals will share similar emotions and experiences at the cost of the loss of the sense of self and empowering them to do things they otherwise would not or could not do (Durkheim 2001; Dornan 2002; Marshall 2002; Throop and Laughlin 2002).

Ritualized practice and knowledge embedded in cultural memory are then expressions of commitment to a group sharing common ethnic/cultural identity. This specific understanding and familiarity of conduct might be a sufficient ground for feeling sameness and bond with those who share this knowledge. Furthermore, participation and active employment of this knowledge reproduces and strengthens the feeling of bond and belonging. Following case study adopts above outlined approaches and focuses on immigrants' employment of cultural memory in ritualized practice.

Early medieval cemeteries on Bornholm

The island of Bornholm is located centrally in the Baltic Sea, between the coast of Sweden, Denmark, Germany and Poland. In the Viking age and early Middle Ages the island was probably independently governed although it was most likely nominally counted to Danish territories. The ties between the island and the Danish rulers were strengthened in the 11th century, which resulted in some significant political and social transformations leading to the reorganization of the administrative system (introduction of parochial system) and the increase of new claims of power. One important dimension of these makeovers was the process of Christianization. Another contemporaneous change in the cultural landscape of the island was influenced by the immigration from the coastal Western Slavic territories. Both these occurrences (i.e. Christianization and inflow of culturally different people) are reflected in the funerary rituals (Naum 2006). In this paper, however, I am interested in highlighting the ritualized practice of the Slavic immigrants.

There are three known and excavated early medieval cemeteries on the island of Bornholm (Fig.1). All of them are located in the south-eastern part of the island, in the area that in the early middle ages (possibly already in Viking Age) formed a sort of administrative, legislative and military unit named in medieval historical sources as Michlingæ herred, which was made up of 256 farms (Nielsen 1998, 13-4, fig.6).

The smallest and most likely the oldest of the graveyards was found in the vicinity of the contemporaneous farm in Runegård, Åker parish (Watt 1985). It is most likely an example of a kin or single farm cemetery as only 27 individuals were buried here. They were lined up in irregular rows in three concentrations - northern with 11 graves, middle section with six exclusively children's graves, and southern group with further nine interments. A single contemporaneous child's grave was found ca 10 m north-east from the burial ground. A large number of burials (11) belonged to children; remaining 14 deceased were adults and juveniles. In slightly more than half of the burials (14 graves) grave goods were registered. The most common objects accompanying the deceased were knives found in nine graves, found alone or in combination with other objects (ceramics, beads, coin). Pots and potsherds were placed in seven graves, beads in three burials and other artifacts - a whetstone, a coin and a belt buckle were found in other graves.

A single find of a coin of Otto-Adelheid type minted sometime between 991 and 1040 as well as pottery shards of both Viking age pottery and Baltic ware helped the excavators to date the cemetery to the late 10th century and the beginnings of the 11th century.

Another early medieval cemetery was found just few hundred metres away from Runegård, adjoining the contemporary settlement of Ndr. Grødbygård. With 525 individuals interred in 515 graves on the surface of 2275 sqm, this is the largest totally excavated cemetery on the island (Wagnkilde 1999; 2000). Ndr. Grødbygård represents a type of cemetery reflecting, most likely, an early parochial organization on Bornholm, which was based on a unit of ca 20 farms. Although no archeologically traceable remains of an enclosure or a church were found, chances are that both these structures were once present and they would not be the only features strongly pointing towards Christian set of standards. As patterned on the other early medieval cemeteries in Scandinavia the graveyard in Ndr. Grødbygård is a row-grave cemetery divided into two zones - northern female and southern male. Majority of the burials were oriented West-East with the heads pointing west. In about 60% of burials coffins of different shape and construction were noticed. What differs Ndr. Grødbygård from contemporary Danish cemeteries (however is consistent with other Bornholm burial ground of this time) is the custom of burying the deceased in full dress and kitting them with common tools. These objects were

found in 61% of burials. Most common were knives that, judging from their placement in the burials, were inserted rather than included in the deceased attire. Other common objects found deposited in the graves included beads (beaded necklaces and head decorations), coins, pots and potsherds. The coins and other objects recovered from burials gave steady dating to the period between ca 1000 and 1100, thus excavators concluded that the Ndr Grødbygård cemetery was established sometime at the beginning of the 11th century and used throughout ca 100 years.

The third cemetery located at Munkegård farm is most likely of similar type as the burial ground in Ndr. Grødbygård. Unfortunately only a part of this cemetery was excavated. A small number of graves were unearthed in the 19th century and another 65 burials were explored in 1997-1999. The excavators calculated that originally there must have been ca 400 graves on total area of ca 1500 sqm. While some interments are still to be excavated, a large southern (male) part of the cemetery was seriously destroyed during road construction in the beginning of the 20th century.

The graves were grouped in more or less regular rows, without traceable external marking, about half of the buried were placed in wooden coffins of various constructions, and majority of deceased were positioned in supine position, along West-East line with their heads towards west. About 70% of burials were equipped. This very high number may not reflect objectively the overall picture of gift giving and burying in the dress, since only female graves were excavated and they usually tend to be 'richer'. Similarly to the other known Bornholm cemeteries from this time, knives are the most commonly encountered objects, followed by beads, coins and pots and potsherds. The cemetery was dated to the 11th century.

The Bornholm early medieval cemeteries merited some attention in Danish archaeology due to unusual ritual practices. Hanne Wagnkilde - the excavator of the Ndr. Grødbygård and Munkegård cemeteries observed that in a number of graves objects originating from the Western Slavic area were deposited.[1] This included knives in the mounted sheaths found in eleven interments in Ndr. Grødbygård and two in Munkegård, silver beads recorded in over 30 interments in Grødbygård and in five in Munkegård, and single examples of temple rings (a form of head decoration) and capsular amulet pendant (so-called 'kaptorga') (Fig.2).

Wagnkilde (2000) argued that these objects, although usually ascribed to the Western Slavic culture do not necessarily point towards migration. She claimed instead that they might be examples of cultural adoptions and inventions resulted from the intensive and mutual trade contacts. She concluded that knife sheath mountings, which are not particularly technologically or stylistically advanced, could have been easily adopted and produced locally. Regarding the silver beads, she rightly pointed out that beads of the same type occur in large numbers in the context of late Viking age and early medieval silver hoards and that they were used as a legal tender. She also concluded that in funerary rituals silver beads might have been regarded as an equivalent of a coin, an object of value, which could be exchanged for other goods (Wagnkilde 2000, 94-7). In her opinion beads, like coins, were most likely a symbolical replacement for other grave goods, and the burials where silver was found might represent a stage between a custom of rich grave gifting with various objects on one hand, and equipment-lacking burials on the other. What is however egregious and not fitting to her theory of silver beads being a replacement for other goods is the fact that not only did all the burials in which these ornaments were found also contain other artifacts (knives, other types of beads, coins, pottery) but also the deceased who wore or were given silver beads, were the most 'equipped' of all buried, at least in Ndr. Grødbygård.

Nonetheless, the silver beads might have simultaneously functioned in both cultural worlds – the one of local inhabitants and the one of Slavic immigrants. They might have had symbolic and biographical meaning for the members of the local elite. Fragmented silver (including beads) was a legal tender circulating between tradesmen. Some of the individuals buried in Ndr. Grødbygård might have been the ones who previously participated in the trade or ones tied with the kinship bonds with those who traveled overseas, thus had access to silver. These beads would function thus as 'an evidence of metaphors for retrospective remembrance' (Williams 2006, 196) evoking other times, but also other places and the journeys made by the deceased's family; these beads would be thus artifacts associated with biography of the deceased as well as their families. The decision to place silver beads with the dead must have been a statement not simply about the personal identity of the deceased but also about the kin group and household, and their social memories. In this case too reference to the idealized and to the past rather than to the real and contemporary order were made.

For the immigrants the meaning embedded in these simple pieces of jewelry might have been different and linked to the perception of proper female body in death. In the circumstances of migration these objects might have received yet another connotation. Material objects and their deposition might have served as a visual measure of difference and a tacit way to communicate the identity of the mourners and the deceased.

---

[1] Although Western Slavic areas in the early Middle Ages are understood as territories east of Saale and Elbe rivers, north of Danube and west of Vistula rivers, in this article I am concerned with the north-western territories of the Slavic culture, particularly these at the Oder estuary (today's north-eastern Germany and north-western Poland).

Commemoration and cultural memory

In some of the interments unearthed on above-mentioned cemeteries, Slavic objects co-occurred with each other, while in others only single examples were found (Fig.3).

In most cases these objects were deposited in analogical way as in burials in the northern parts of the Western Slavic area, i.e. in the territory the suspected immigrant might have come from. The knives in the mounted sheaths were either attached to the deceased belt or placed by the body; beads were parts of the necklaces or found in the head area indicating their use as headband ornaments, as was the case with a temple ring; potsherds of Baltic ware were places at the limits of the grave pit, scattered around the body or cast in the soil covering the graves. Some objects, however, seem to be used incorrectly. This is particularly striking in the case of female jewelry, where earrings' beads are found worn on the neck, a temple ring was turned into a brooch, beads that were originally a part of necklaces where found in the head area. This might be indication of local appropriation of these pieces of jewelry. Also temple rings, which were most frequent piece of jewelry found in the contemporaneous interments in the Western Slavic area, were virtually absent from the deceased dress code in Bornholm interments. Instead silver beads were preferred. Interestingly, it could be speculated that this dress appropriation might have been restrained only to the burial rituals. In the context of contemporaneous settlement sites thoroughly surveyed with metal detectors, single finds of silver beads are extremely rare, instead a number of temple rings were registered!

The use of jewelry and other elements of dress in the funerary rituals lead to highlighting two important aspects of identity and cultural memory, the significance of material aspect of cultural memory and the importance of the body and dress in establishing and maintaining cultural identity.

Body is inseparably connected with dress and ornamentation. As noted by Entwistle, dress 'is an intimate aspect of the experience and presentation of the self and is so closely linked to identity that these three - dress, the body and the self - are not perceived separately but simultaneously, as a totality' (Entwistle 2000, 10). Dress and the body are often key aspects in immigrant - host discourse because the practice of costume and body are the areas where differences can be overtly played out without verbal communication. In this way dress could become a visual measure of difference. It is a central means by which identities become somatically informed and grounded and a form of body memory. In the circumstances of funeral the use of culturally specific objects could have yet another purpose. One has to remember that funerary rituals were conducted as much for the deceased as for the living collective of mourners. And as funerals were often gatherings not excluded to the participation of the closest and initiated ones, the onlookers, who observed the funeral rituals, thought and wondered, indeed also participated in this event.

For immigrants the silver beads, temple rings, amulets and knives in the mounted sheaths might have been a visual marking of familiarity, material aspect of memory and concrete past tenaciously employed in ritual situation. Objects then could potentially work here as means of shaping cultural personhood of the dead with reference to the times before migrations. If the memory of the past before migration mattered and if migration was used as an event conclusive for identity construction, memory of origins might have been captured into cultural forms in a struggle against oblivion. Objects might be granted particular significance and evocative strength as they can encapsulate meaning connected with the past. As such they serve as vehicle for expression and materialization of cultural memory and identity. Through rituals and manipulation of the material culture references to the past and the idealized state of things can be made. To quote Rowlands (1993, 144), 'Objects are culturally constructed to connote and consolidate the possessions of past events associated with their use and ownership. They are there to be talked about and invested with the memories and striking events associated with their use. The link between past, present and future is made through their materiality'.

However in the case of Bornholm early medieval cemeteries it is not only the occurrence and use of dress that might indicate a separate group identity of immigrant Slavs. There are other practices that should be related to ritual practice of immigrants, like the use of pottery. In number of graves in Runegård, Munkegård and Ndr. Grødbygård potsherds of Baltic ware were found among the objects deposited in the graves and in the soil covering the graves. The excavator of the Runegård burial ground noticed their appearance with surprise as this custom of *pars pro toto* is not known from Scandinavia in the Viking age and early Middle Ages (Watt 1985, 93). In some cases pottery shards and complete pots are of a visibly worse technological and aesthetic quality and in single cases miniature cups were found. All of these practices regarding ceramics are known from the 10th-11th century cemeteries recorded south of the Baltic Sea (Hollnagel 1960; Wojtasik 1968; Bulska and Wrzesińscy 1996). It is even more remarkable that in Runegård the deceased that were given whole pots (usually children who were offered handmade Viking age pots) are buried in a different zone than those who were given potsherds (Fig.4). This zoning and variation in ritual could be an overlooked indication of diverse system of norms and identities among Runegård inhabitants. It might be also a reflection of immigrant exclusion either dictated by the host groups, owners of the farm or chosen by the immigrants themselves. Cultural and maybe social disparity could led them to the preference to burry the closest ones and adherents of the same ideas next to each

other, hence the visible division in the cemetery.

Differences in use of pottery in funerary ceremonies are also visible in the case of two other cemeteries although they lack the clear zoning observed in Runegård.

There is yet another phenomenon worth exploring in the context of ritual response of immigrants. The analysis of the three cemeteries provides a ground for hypothesis about possible shifts in ritual behavior of immigrants due to the changes in cultural memory. It has to be stated, however that changes in cultural memory not always meant a shift in self-description and identification with a group, at least not in the straightforward fashion.

Rituals, although built upon mythic logics, could undergo certain modifications and reformulations. Some ritual practices, like the immigrants' funerary practice in this case, are rather infrequently transmitted. Thus for a long periods of time the details of rituals are stored in memory, and as most likely a subject of taboo, they are rarely discussed. Thus each reproduction of the ritual might differ in various ways from the last as a direct result of failing or distorting memories. Such shifts occur unconsciously and are unrecognized. However, modification or elimination of any particular process or element of ritual, which is being irregularly transmitted, whether due to memory failure or some other specific cause, does not substantially undermine continuity in the tradition as a whole. Furthermore, the emotions involved in ritual that are partly associated with the physical realities of death, i.e. disappearing of the social being and appearance of a lifeless cadaver, and partly with the transcendent states of the decease, the uncertainty of after-life reality, may be regarded as powerful mnemonic devices, greatly reducing the risk of forgetting and thus of the unconscious or unintended introduction of innovations. Nonetheless, even when ritual practice undergoes conscious changes, every shift and newly established authoritative version of ritualized conduct has to be within certain frames, so it continues to be familiar for a group and continues to guarantee the effect of 'collective effervescence'.

The possible shifts in ritual response of the immigrant seem most apparent in the case of Ndr. Grødbygård cemetery, where hypothetical assumptions about changes in ritual can be made from the spatial arrangement of the cemetery. In the female zone interments where a few Slavic objects or practices were combined with each other tend to be grouped in the center, i.e. in most likely the oldest part of this zone. The graves located towards the extremes of the northern zone (hence the youngest ones) show propensity of changes in the dress and the sole element that could be with some certainty associated with immigrants are potsherds and maybe pots placed with the deceased. Thus, if the assumption about relationship between spatiality and chronology is correct, that is if the cemetery grew from the center towards extremes, a general conclusion could be made about changes in the rituals throughout the time. For the same reason it is interesting to study clustered graves with foreign objects and traces of foreign rituals. One such cluster is made up of four female graves located in the central part of the northern zone of the cemetery (graves 426 - 429) (Fig.5). In the three overlapping graves women were given almost exact sets of ornaments and gifts consisting of beaded necklaces including the same type of silver beads in two graves, knives (one in mounted sheath) and coins. In another grouping of five female graves (545, 558-561) (Fig.6) elements of dress and grave gifts differ in every interments, yet in four of them there is at least one trait pointing towards Slavic tradition - temple ring, silver beads, potsherds of the Baltic ware. In yet another grouping of seven graves (graves 27, 28, 607-609, 615, 3), which is lacking stratigraphical relation, all women buried next to each other were given knives and beaded necklaces or at least single beads, three of them were additionally given a pot and one a potshard. One of these women, besides a knife, beads and pot was given two amulets - an animal tooth and capsular pendant called 'kaptorga'.

Some of the above mentioned and other clusters, in the context of which foreign objects and practices were recorded, show rather a static tendency in the choice of objects and their treatment or at least in the principle of these practices, while the others show a propensity of changes in ceremonies, especially with regards to dress. Generally, the younger the interment the material elements of attire, particularly jewelry, become less distinctive and less ethnically or culturally charged. If indeed these clusters represent the burials of female immigrants, they would indicate changes in ritual with regards to presentation of the body.

Williams (2006) observed a similar tendency on some of the early medieval cemeteries in Britain. He argued that a slight change in deposition and selection of artifacts in graves looks as if mourners aimed at purposeful evoking the past through re-enacting the earlier burial rite, and also at making a distinctive image against which the earlier interments were played off but not replicated. 'Each individual burial was a ritual performance serving not only to create a memorable image of the deceased, but also to respond to and evoke earlier interments through burial rites and location. This image production and image reproduction combined to sustain the mortuary tradition and create links between the living, the recently dead, and possible concept of ancestry and ancestors through the use of grave goods in the funeral' (Williams 2006, 62).

Summary

In the present paper I attempted at linking phenomena of identity formation and shaping with the notion of cultural memory. I argued that funerary rituals being a component of cultural memory and exteriorized knowledge build upon mythic logics and being bridges through which past is carried to the present are of particular significance for reinforcing the feeling of identity and relatedness. It is because the employment and participation in ritual goes beyond verbal expression. Funerary rituals, like any other rites, are specialized practices, enactment of which is based on the common mnemonic knowledge of how to execute them correctly. They are employed in one of the most traumatic circumstances in human life - death and vanishing of an individual, family and community member. As such they are stimulating emotional response allowing participants to identify with one another in sharing an explicit sense of purpose, creating social unity, supporting and validating the collective sense of group membership. It is through such a dual working of practical experience and cultural memories that identities are constituted and maintained.

Another important argument presented in this paper relates to the significance and evocative strength of the objects employed in the circumstances of ritual. I argued that material culture was a vehicle for expression and materialization of cultural memory and identity. They are mediated by and through material culture, not least through dress and body ornamentation. Objects are infused with capacities to endure time, with meaning exciding their function to retain fragments of the past in the present.

Finally, I tried to show that even though ritual knowledge is build upon mythical logics, the enactment of ritual could nevertheless undergo certain shifts and reformulations. These shifts, as long as agreed upon by the members of a group, do not necessarily cause a split in group's awareness of unity and particularity. I also argued that in situation of migration, the social and cultural circumstances, the immigrants and their offspring are placed in, may lead to more or less rapid socialization with the 'mnemonic other' host group and acquirement of their collective memory.

References

Assmann, J., 2006. *Religion and Cultural Memory*, Stanford.

Assmann, J., 1995. 'Collective Memory and Cultural Identity', *New German Critique* 65, 125-33.

Barth, F., 1969. 'Introduction', *Ethnic Groups and Boundaries*, F. Barth (ed.), Boston, 9-38.

Bloch, M., 1996. 'Internal and External Memory. Different Ways of Being in History', *Tense Past. Cultural Essays in Trauma and Memory*, P. Antze and M. Lambek (eds.), New York, 216-232.

Bulska, E., Wrzesińscy, A. and Wrzesińscy, J., 1996. 'Zawartość naczyń grobowych – próba analizy i interpretacji', *Studia Lednickie IV*, 345-56.

De Vos, G. and Romanussi-Ross, L., 1995. 'Ethnic Identity, A Psychocultural Perspective', *Ethnic Identity. Creation, Conflict, and Accommodation*, L. Romanucci-Ross and G. De Voss (eds.), Walnut Creek, 349-380.

Dornan, J. 2002. 'Agency and Archaeology, Past, Present, and Future Directions', *Journal of Archaeological Method and Theory* 9.4, 303-29.

Durkheim, E. 2001 [1912]. *The Elementary Forms of Religious Life*, Oxford.

Entwistle, J. 2000. *The Fashioned Body. Fashion, Dress and Modern Social Theory*, Cambridge.

Hollnagel, A. 1960. 'Das slawische Körpergräberfeld von Gustaväl, Kreis Sternberg, mit einem Anhang über die slawischen Grabfunde in Mecklenburg', *Bodenkmalpflege in Mecklenburg*, 127-68.

Jones, S. 1997. *The Archaeology of Ethnicity*, London.

Lambek, M. and Antze, P., 1996. 'Introduction. Forecasting Memory', in, *Tense Past. Cultural Essays in Trauma and Memory*, P. Antze and M. Lambek (eds.), New York, xi-xxxvii.

Marshall, D.A., 2002. 'Behavior, Belonging, and Belief, A Theory of Ritual Practice', *Sociological Theory* 20.3, 360-80.

Naum, M. 2006. 'Early Christians, immigrants and ritualized practice. A case study of South-eastern Bornholm', *Lund Archaeological Review* 11-2, 17-36.

Nielsen, F.O., 1988. *Middelalderens Bornholm*, Ronne.

Olick, J. 1999. 'Collective Memory, The Two Cultures', *Sociological Theory* 17.3, 333-48.

Olick, J. and Robbins, J., 1998. 'Social Memory Studies, From "Collective Memory" to the Historical Sociology of Mnemonic Practices', *Annual Review of Sociology* 24, 105-40.

Olsen, B. and Kobyliński, Z., 1991. 'Ethnicity in anthropological and archaeological research, a Norwegian-Polish perspective', *Archaeologia Polona* 29, 5-27.

Rouse, R., 1995. 'Questions of Identity, Personhood and Collectivity in Transnational Migration to the United States', *Critique of Anthropology* 15, 351-80.

Rowlands, M., 1993. 'The role of memory in the transmission of culture', *World Archaeology* 25.2, 141-51.

Throop, J. and Laughlin, C.D., 2002. 'Ritual, Collective Effervescence and the Categories,

Toward a Neo-Durkheimian Model of the Nature of Human Consciousness, Feeling and Understanding', *Journal of Ritual Studies* 16.1, 40-63.

Wagnkilde, H., 1999. 'Slaviske træk i bornholmske grave fra tiden omkring kristendommens indførelse. En oversigt over gravpladser og skattefund fra 1000 tallet på Bornholm', *META* 2, 3-20.

Wagnkilde, H., 2000. 'Gravudstyr og mønter fra 1000-tallets gravpladser på Bornholm', *Hikuin* 27, 91-106.

Watt, M. 1985. 'En gravplads fra sen vikingetid ved Runegård, Åker', *Fra Bornholms Museum* 1984-1985, 77-100.

Wojtasik, J. 1968. *Cmentarzysko wczesnośredniowieczne na wzgórzu „Młynówka" w Wolinie*, Szczecin.

Yelvington, K. 1991. 'Ethnicity as Practice? A Comment on Bentley', *Comparative Studies in Society and History* 33.1, 158-168.

Zerubavel, E. 1996. 'Social Memories, Step to a Sociology of the Past', *Qualitative Sociology* 19.3, 283-99.

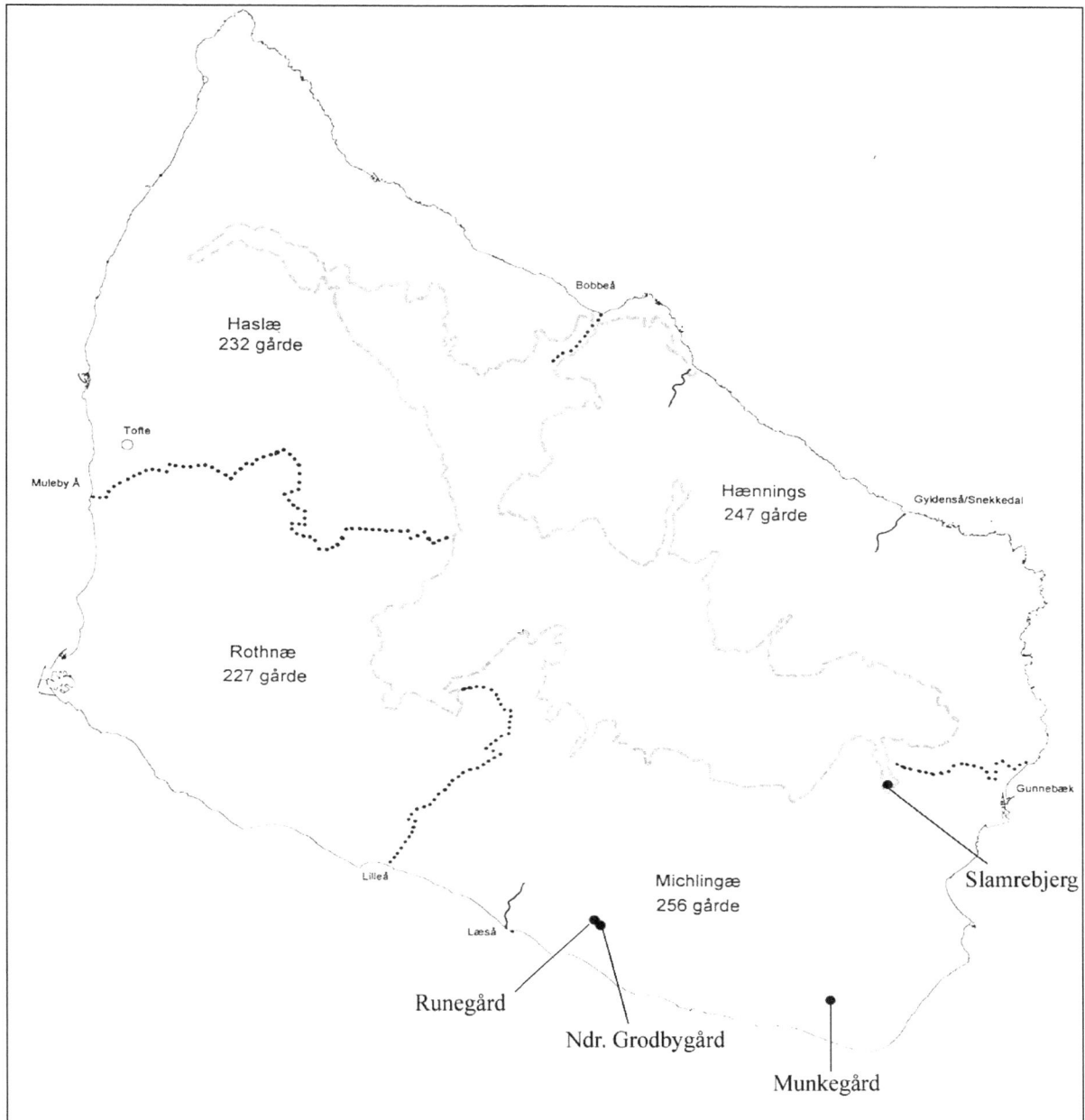

Figure 1. Early medieval administrative division of Bornholm and the location of the studied cemeteries (after Nielsen, 1998, 14).

Figure 2. Examples of Slavic objects found in Ndr. Grødbygård and Munkegård. From upper left: silver bead-pendant; silver openwork bead from a basket-shaped earring (re-used as a necklace bead); silver bead decorated with granulation from a necklace; silver round, filigree bead from an earring turned into a necklace bead; bronze knife sheath mounting; silver temple ring turned into a brooch (photo: author).

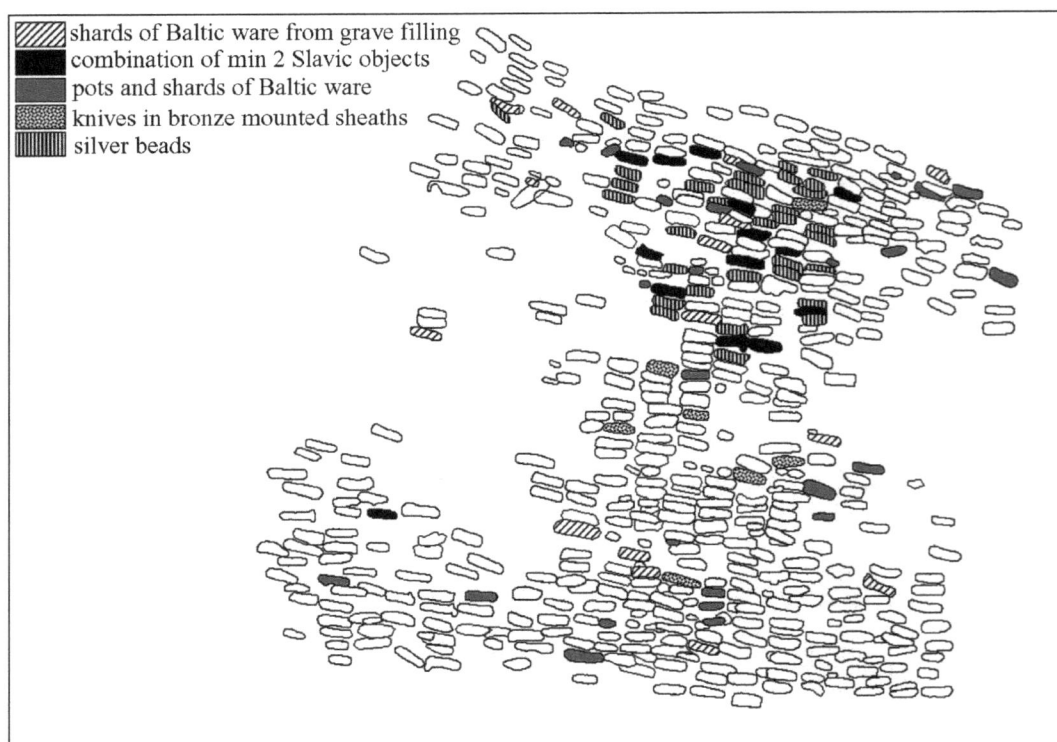

Figure 3. Objects and rituals associated with Slavic tradition observed on Ndr. Grødbygård cemetery.

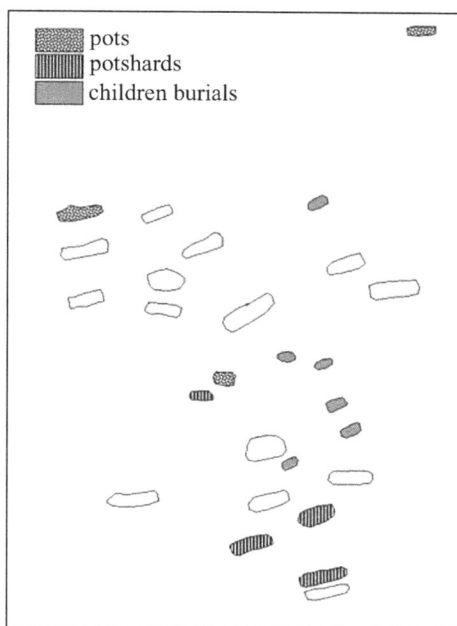

Figure 4. Differences in use of pottery in Runegård cemetery

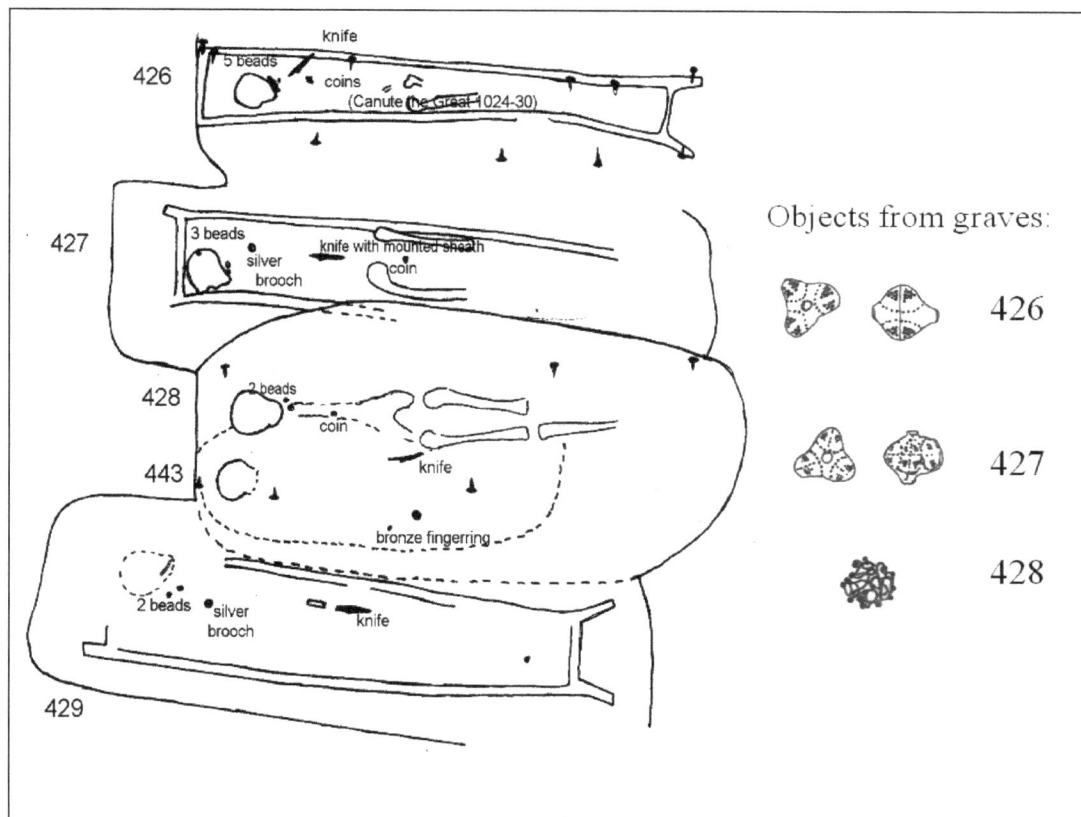

Figure 5. Example of stratigraphically related female interments from Ndr. Grødbygård with similar depositions of objects, including silver beads of Slavic origins.

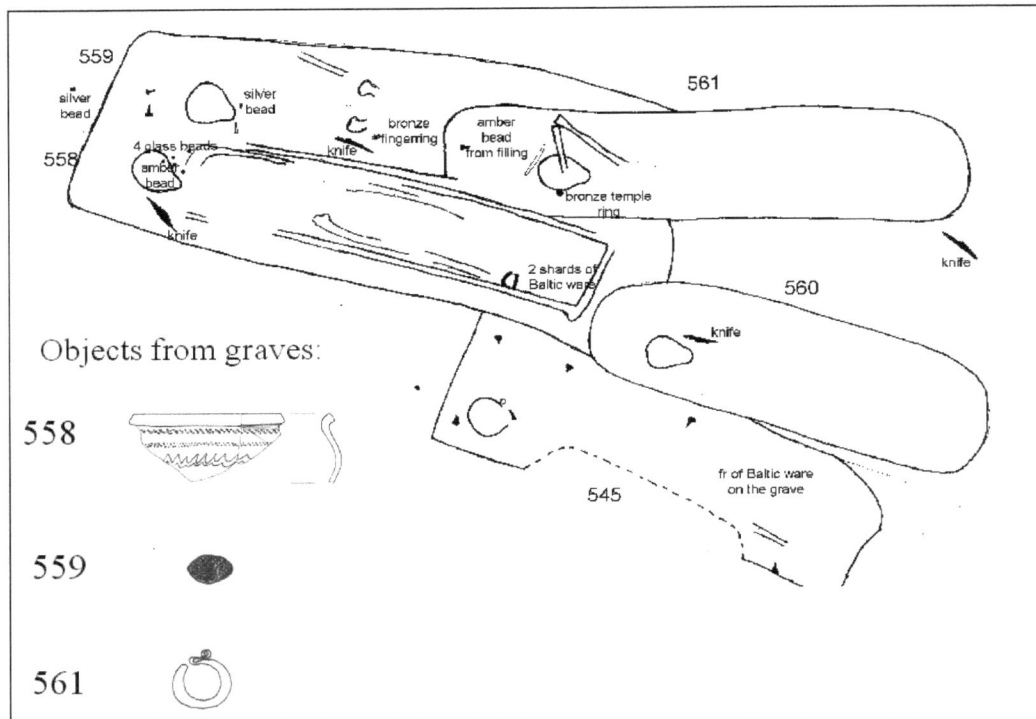

Figure 6. Example of stratigraphically related female interments from Ndr. Grødbygård. In four interments, 545, 558, 559 and 561 there is at least one trait pointing towards Slavic tradition - temple ring, silver beads, potsherds of the Baltic ware.

The Branding of Minoan Archaeology ™

Anna Simandiraki, Trevor Grimshaw

Introduction

Crete is the largest Greek island. In the absence of deciphered records, our knowledge of its Minoan civilisation (3rd - 2nd millennia BC) derives almost exclusively from its material culture. 'Minoan Archaeology', therefore, is a term with two meanings. On the one hand, it refers to the materiality of the Minoan civilisation. On the other hand, it refers to the group of practitioners and practices that have examined this field during the past 100 or so years. This duality will be retained throughout the chapter.

Several recent studies have sought to address the processes by which Minoan archaeology constructs its identity; the ways in which it relates to modernity; and the possibilities for reflective engagement with its processes and artifacts (Bintliff 1984; Hamilakis 1999; 2002; Preziosi 2002; Hitchcock and Koudounaris 2002; Brown and Hamilakis 2003; Solomon 2003; 2005; 2006a; 2006b; Papadopoulos 2005; Cherry *et al.* 2005; Hamilakis and Momigliano 2006). However, despite being invaluable and innovative, such studies have yet to make a considerable impact on 'mainstream' Minoan archaeology, as reflected in the bulk of published research. The latter is still largely preoccupied with materiality and tends to regard everything else as peripheral. Moreover, recent developments in archaeological thought and practice, such as archaeological ethnographies (Joyce 2002; Edgeworth 2006; Holtorf 2007), have yet to be applied in a Minoan archaeological context. By contributing this paper we seek to address this significant gap in the literature.

We believe that reflexive approaches to Minoan archaeology need to be further pursued and reinforced. In particular, we believe that the institutionalised ways in which Minoan archaeology is currently produced and consumed should be subjected to a constructive critique. Furthermore, understanding how archaeological identities are constructed may provide insights into the micropolitics of the discipline, a subject which has hitherto been treated as taboo. We hope that this will result in better opportunities for those who are disenfranchised by current practices.

This chapter forms part of an ongoing project by the authors, some aspects of which have already been communicated elsewhere.[1] The

---

[1] Previous versions / aspects of this paper include: Grimshaw T. and Simandiraki A. 2006, *The branding of academic knowledge: an archaeological case study,* paper presented at the BAAL/IRAAL Annual Conference, 'From Applied Linguistics to Linguistics Applied: Issues, Practices, Trends', Cork, Ireland, 7-9 September 2006; Simandiraki A. 2006, *The branding of Minoan archaeology,* paper presented at the European Association of Archaeologists 12th Annual Meeting, Cracow, Poland, 19-24 September 2006; Simandiraki A. 2006, *Minoan archaeology in modern Cretan administration,* paper presented at the 10th International Cretological Congress, Chania, Crete, Greece, 1-8 October 2006; Simandiraki A. 2006, *To*

project aims to investigate micropolitical and discursive aspects of Minoan Archaeology, building on reflexive approaches such as the ones outlined above. This research stems from our common interest in the discursive construction of individuals and communities, including professional academic communities. Our research uses a multi-method approach, which to date has included the following,

- Multi-modal discourse analysis of a range of artefacts, including academic publications (books, articles); excavation interim reports; educational materials (Simandiraki 2004; 2005; 2006); commercial products (Fig.1); tourist brochures (Fig.3); course prospectuses; guidebooks (Fig.6); newspaper publications (including advertisements); public lecture posters; job advertisements; museum and site exhibitions; and electronic resources.
- Ethnographic observations conducted at the Palace of Knossos, focusing on linguistic aspects and on the activities of museum guides.
- Ethnographic observations of public ceremonies, focusing on the reproduction and appropriation of Minoan material by

---

display or to forget: a false dichotomy?, paper presented at the Theoretical Archaeology Group conference, Exeter, U.K., 15-17 December 2006; Simandiraki A. 2007, *Kings, axes, palaces, dolphins: Minoan archaeology as Cretan, Greek and European identity,* poster presented at "Re-visioning the Nation: Cultural Heritage and the Politics of Disaster", The 8th Cambridge Heritage Seminar, Cambridge, U.K., 12 May 2007. A short contribution, Simandiraki A., Grimshaw T. in press, *Linguistic Imperialism and Minoan Archaeology,* is scheduled to appear in the Forum section of Archaeologies (the World Archaeological Congress journal). Simandiraki A. in press, *Minoan archaeology in modern Cretan administration,* will be published in the Proceedings of the 10th International Cretological Congress. The ideas presented herein have also been explored in A.Simandiraki's teaching.

the public domain (Simandiraki 2005; 2006).

- Interviews with archaeologists and members of the public.
- Reflexive journals (kept over a period of 13 years) in which we have recorded and reflected on fieldwork; museum micropolitics; job allocation; and the process of academic publication.

We do not intend this as an exhaustive account of identity construction within Minoan archaeology. Nor do we refute other approaches. Instead, we seek to complement them. Our guiding questions are,

a) How can the concept of branding inform our understanding of the construction of people, artefacts, cultural knowledge and practices related to Minoan archaeology?

b) Can awareness of the branding of Minoan archaeology in the commercial and community domains illuminate similar practices in the academic domain?

Before addressing these questions, let us first consider our conceptual framework.

Theoretical framework

The theoretical basis of our study is the concept of *discourse*. The definition of discourse that we will follow is that which has in recent years become common within the social sciences. Thus,

> 'A discourse refers to a set of meanings, metaphors, representations, images, stories, statements and so on that in some way together produce a particular creation of events. It refers to a particular picture that is painted of an event (or person or class of persons), a particular way of representing it or them in a certain light' (Burr 1995, 48).

In choosing this sociological definition of discourse we wish to distance ourselves from the common understanding of discourse as a 'talk', a 'treatise' or a 'series of utterances' (Oxford English Dictionary 2007). It should be noted that within this theoretical field a *text* is seen as the physical, symbolic manifestation of a discourse. While discourse is the process, text is the product. Furthermore, the term *text* refers not only to written language but to anything that can be 'read' for meaning, including pictures, architecture and other aspects of material culture (Burr 1995, 51).

Recent social theory sees life as characterised by competing discourses, with individuals and groups making representations and seeking acceptance for their constructions of the world. Some examples include 'the discourses of democracy, law, capitalism, socialism, education, linguistics, applied linguistics and so on' (Pennycook 1994, 128). Some others which are relevant to the discipline of archaeology would be the discourses of processualism, postprocessualism, island archaeologies etc.

Discourses influence our ways of thinking by controlling the meanings available to us. They classify and organise knowledge, producing a 'symbolic order' around which we construct our social lives. They also define the criteria by which we make judgements; e.g. what is considered right or wrong, rational or irrational (Bilton *et al.* 1996, 96). In all areas of social life it is possible to discern a *dominant discourse*, a way of perceiving the world which tends to be accepted as 'common sense' by the majority of members of the relevant community.

It is important to understand discursive practice as a two-way process. On the one hand, social actors are able to master and manipulate discourses, therefore writing themselves into the social world. On the other hand, the social world then turns around and, through the medium of discourses, creates constraints upon its members (Usher and Edwards 1994, 28). Discursive practice is thus an intrinsic feature of the agency-structure dialectic.

The work of one researcher has been particularly influential in raising consciousness of discourse as social practice and offering a methodological approach for its investigation. Fairclough's (1995) Critical Discourse Analysis involves two dimensions. The first is a relatively conventional form of linguistic analysis, focussing on aspects such as the vocabulary, semantics and grammar of a spoken or written text. The second is intertextual analysis, which concerns the ways in which social actors borrow from texts (in the aforementioned wider sense) in order to create other texts. This also implies the blending and mixing of discourses and genres.

Within the discipline of archaeology we may find at least two examples which serve as illustrations of intertextuality. One of these is stratigraphy. When archaeologists examine a cross-section of soil, they interpret the accumulated layers as representing different periods of time. Their reading of this physical data is a form of intertextual analysis. Another example is a palimpsest. This was the result of a process whereby successive layers of text were written one on top of another on medieval parchments. Archaeologists' ability to read these multiple layers on the same surface is another form of intertextual analysis.

Texts have an inherent historicity (Fairclough 1992, 102). They accumulate meanings over time, as they are reinterpreted by successive generations (Simandiraki 2004, 181-5). Critical analysis enables us to trace the chain of references that have been inscribed upon them along the way. It can also reveal how the resources of the past are exploited in order to serve the needs of the present.

In recent years critical discourse approaches have been applied across a range of professional-academic communities, showing them to be constituted by discursive practices; i.e. shared systems of taxonomic knowledge, interactional resources and analytic frameworks which shape and constrain their conceptual environment. Mastery of the locally dominant discourse normalizes interpretations and sets the conditions for inclusion/exclusion. Language is a key modality of this discourse, serving as both the medium of socialization and the principal mode of representation.

We now turn our attention to branding, which is a particular type of discursive practice. Again, the work of Fairclough (1995) provides a useful framework for our understanding of the issues. Fairclough (1995) examines the commodification and marketisation of discourse across a wide range of domains, within the broad context of a consumer society. In particular, he focuses on the colonisation of academic discourse by fields such as advertising and management. The restructuring of discourse practices is evident in texts such as university prospectuses and academic job descriptions. In recent years these have been increasingly influenced by practices associated with advertising, including the blending of information and persuasion and the interactive combination of diverse symbolic forms, especially language and visual images (Preziosi 2002; Keller 2003, 596; Askegaard 2006; Balmer 2006, 35, 36-8).

In general terms, 'the ideological work of advertising' has three dimensions, (a) the building of relations between the consumer and the vendor; (b) the building of images; and (c) the building of the consumer; i.e. the fact that we are all constructed as consumers, regardless of whether or not we wish to be (Fairclough 1989, 199-211). Branding relates to the second of these dimensions. Within the literatures of marketing and management this refers to the construction of a consistent identity through verbal, visual, attitudinal and other strategies (Fairclough 1989, 199-211; Schroeder and Salzer-Morling, 2006). It serves to promote products and services. It is based on key concepts such as loyalty, quality, longevity, pride and reliability. It is associated with in-group behaviour and exclusivity. It involves producers, consumers and vendors; although it should be noted that these categories overlap, since a person can perform more than one role at the same time. It should also be noted that when a consumer is loyal to a brand this may not necessarily be because the product is of good quality, but simply because the consumer feels proud of it and wishes to be associated with it.

In this paper we wish to stress that the concept of branding has implications that extend far beyond its origins within the field of marketing. As members of late capitalist society, we are all familiar with certain commercial brands that are associated with fast food companies, fashion houses or cars. But the notion of branding is also applicable to governmental organisations, institutions, and even specific individuals. For instance, a national flag operates as a brand in that it seeks to construct an identity and to command loyalty through visual symbolism.

Having outlined our conceptual framework, we will now concentrate on our specific topic, the branding of Minoan archaeology. In the remainder of this paper we will consider some examples of the different forms of branding (commercial, community and academic). We will finish with some conclusions and recommendations.

Minoan Archaeology and Branding

Minoan archaeology, like other archaeologies, is constructed through discourses. This discursive construction is achieved through the examination and representation of particular artefacts, both in academic and non-academic domains. Some of the most popular artefacts have been adopted in such a way that they have become stereotypical icons, or 'fossils' (Simandiraki 2004, 181-4). Given that our subsequent discussion will refer to the use of such 'fossils' in commercial and community branding, it is useful to remind the reader that the most well-known of these include, the Prince of Lilies fresco; Evans's reconstruction of the North West Propylon; the Toreador Fresco; the Knossos 'Throne Room' (also called 'the first throne in Europe'); the Blue Ladies fresco; and 'Minoan' names from Classical mythology, e.g. Minos, Minotaur, Ariadne, Kydon. Let us now turn to specific areas of Minoan branding.

Minoan branding and commerce

We will begin by considering how Minoan archaeology is discursively constructed through the process of commercial branding. This involves the employment of Minoan materiality chiefly for monetary gain. Classic examples include the use of artefacts and monuments as logos for brands of food and drink. Minoan commercial branding is overt and mainly connected to tourism (Figs 1-2). Herakleion experiences the bulk of Minoan-related tourism due to Knossos and the city's Archaeological Museum. Simply by wandering around these sites one can see a range of Minoan appropriations, from the names of tavernas and other local businesses ('Pasiphae', 'Minotaur') to machine-woven rugs bearing the Toreador Fresco. Such cases of the commercial branding of Minoan archaeology are too numerous to mention. Here we will cite only two.

Let us take the example of Fig.1, the label on a bottle of Cretan wine. This employs the North West Propylon of the Palace of Knossos as a visual logo. This architectural feature has been established in the public domain as a calcified form of cultural heritage (Simandiraki 2004; Solomon 2006). As such, it plays a vital role in the discursive construction of the Minoan civilisation. It also holds an iconic significance within the

narrative and public memory of Evans' excavation of Knossos. In other words, the image brands the Minoan civilisation for having produced it; and it brands Evans for having excavated and reconstructed it. The picture on the label of the bottle is combined with the word 'Knossos' in a way that is characteristic of advertising (Fairclough 1989). The association of the modern wine with a prehistoric artefact and a Classical word creates a narrative of continuity and tradition. But this use of an iconic artefact is not a blind or contingent appropriation. As several authors have pointed out, Minoan archaeology is constantly being reinvented, reinterpreted, and re-cast into new narratives (Simandiraki 2004; 2005; Askegaard 2006, 97; Hamilakis 2006; Solomon 2006). Such narratives are created through the interweaving of multiple discourses, including those of consumerism, politics and patriotism. In consuming the wine, the buyers simultaneously satisfy their own local, patriotic and emotional loyalties. Thus, the bottle, the wine, the North West Propylon and Knossos cease to be mere commodities. They serve as a brand for local pride, Cretanness and Greekness. The become part of a perpetuated tradition.

Another example is the entry tickets to the Knossos Palace (Fig.2). These pieces of paper, issued by the Ministry of Culture, depict the Palace's most famous locus, the 'Throne Room'; in fact Evans's reconstruction of this room. As such, they serve as official, tangible representations of the site. By buying a ticket the visitor buys a whole package of cultural associations (Solomon 2006, 172-3). Another way of putting this is to say that the ticket simultaneously brands the site, the visitor, the Ministry, the island of Crete and Minoan archaeology. Moreover, the tourist who retains his/her ticket as a souvenir of the visit becomes part of the historicity of the site (Solomon 2006, 170, 178). Similarly, when that visitor has his/her photograph taken in front of one of the monuments, s/he becomes part of the discourse of Minoan archaeology. S/he 'writes her/himself into the discourse'.

Minoan branding and community

Let us now consider the case of community branding in Minoan archaeology, which may partly overlap with commercial branding. We define community branding as the employment of Minoan materiality chiefly for the construction of the identity of a community. This type of branding manifests itself not only in tourism but also in areas such as local Cretan administration (Simandiraki in press) and formal or semi-formal public performances (Hamilakis 2006).

One example of this is currency, a form of state branding. Coins have borne images and fictions of the Minoan civilisation, filtered through Ancient Greek mythology, since Classical antiquity. For example, Knossian coins of the Classical era depicted the Minotaur and the Labyrinth to convey an image of Knossos as a mythical city and to create its identity as a sovereign state. In more recent times, an emergency note issued by the Greek State in 1941 (during the Nazi occupation) depicts the Blue Ladies Minoan fresco (recto) and a Minoan column (verso). Also, the last 500 drachma note issued by the Greek State (before the introduction of the Euro) depicted another Minoan Knossian artefact, a faience plaque of a goat suckling its kids (verso).

Another case of local Cretan administration employing Minoan materiality for branding purposes are semi-official publications, such as the tourist brochure for Herakleion published by its Municipality (Fig.3). Like the local brand of wine (see above), the brochure uses the North West Propylon from Knossos as a readily identifiable logo. It also features Minoan dolphins in its decorative borders; and various other Minoan elements throughout, including the Toreador fresco. All of these 'fossils' co-exist in a palimpsest of materialities and narratives, combining to create cultural continuity. Such publications serve to maintain local identity and promote Crete as 'the birthplace of Europe' in the collective consciousness of a wider national or international audience.

Adaptations of Minoan materiality can also be observed in 20th century architecture, both public and private (Hamilakis 2006, 9.3, 9.4, 9.6; Solomon 2006, fig.10.6). The best example is the 'Minoan' Heroon in Herakleion, which was built in the 1930s and was intended as a symbol of local identity (Cadogan 2004; Simandiraki in press). It reproduces Evans's reconstructions of Minoan architecture. That is to say, it expresses the public's construct of what the Minoans would build, though not necessarily what they actually did build. A further example is the Herakleion Prefecture Headquarters Building, the administrative seat for the whole region. This consists of a combination of mostly Neoclassical and early 20th century architecture, with further prominent 'iconic' Minoan double axes embellishing the ironwork on its doors and windows. This building is part of a more extensive complex which includes the local police headquarters and the Law Courts.

The interior furnishings of public buildings reproduce the same tropes. A suite of furniture in the office of the Prefect of Chania is an interesting example of the appropriation of Minoan Archaeology as a symbol of Cretan administration. This was reputedly supplied to the office in the 1950s (pers. com. 1996), but it has since been rearranged. It comprised one sizeable desk, two archive cabinets and several chairs (the latter now missing). All were made by traditional local carpenters. One cabinet (Fig.4) depicts large double axes; the other depicts two heraldic Princes of Lilies (which occupy almost the entire height of the cabinet door). The desk is the most impressive of the three pieces. It is covered in references to Minoan culture, including double axes, a bull's head and an imitation of a Classical Knossian coin bearing the Minotaur.

Street names in Cretan cities are also indicative of how Minoan archaeology, as materiality and as a discipline, is used in local administration. They include the names of real Minoan sites (e.g. Knossos, Juktas); mythical people and places (e.g. Minos, the Labyrinth); and even Minoan archaeologists (e.g. Evans, Platon). Occasionally, street signs include explanations in Greek under these names. For example, Evans is described as an 'English Archaeologist of Knossos'. This reinforces the connection between Evans and Knossos, but obscures other discourses with which this man was associated during his lifetime. This fusion of identities creates a palimpsest that is retained and reproduced in public memory.

Formal or semi-formal public performances also play a vital role in the discursive construction of Cretan modernity as a successor of Minoan materiality (Simandiraki 2005; 2006; Hamilakis 2006). An interesting case was the public ceremonies that took place during the Athens 2004 Olympic Games (Fig.5) (Solomon 2006, fig.10.8). Through the use of visual narratives, these created connections between Minoan archaeology and the ancient Olympic Games. For example, during a procession at the opening ceremony, depictions of Minoan games derived from archaeological materiality were linked to depictions of the Classical games in a visual continuum, although these links are not supported by archaeological evidence (Simandiraki 2005). In other words, the ceremony imposed upon the spectators a non-archaeological discourse of archaeology. Meanwhile, the event in its entirety served to reproduce and reinforce the construct of a Greek national identity (Wodak *et al.* 1999). Similar instances of the appropriation and reformulation of Minoan archaeology within a modern narrative can be observed in educational contexts, such as school plays

and enactments of frescoes by schoolchildren (Simandiraki 2006).

It is important to recognise the part that individual social actors play in the discursive construction and subsequent transmission of cultural identities. For example, through exposure to 'fossils' of the Minoan civilisation the people who work in or visit municipal buildings are inscribed by powerful discourses of Cretan identity. In this way they develop a sense of loyalty to the local culture, which they may subsequently express in other contexts. So, the physical environment operates as a structural reproducer of discourses of cultural heritage; but these discourses are activated through the agency of members of the culture, thereby contributing to the collective memory. Similarly, those who participate in the aforementioned public performances play an active role (quite literally) in the reproduction of cultural traditions. In both cases there are clear parallels with the notion of brand loyalty. Moreover, by actually participating in a ceremony and being seen to participate (as opposed to remaining a spectator or simply publishing a newspaper article about it) the individual engages in a form of personal branding. We will examine further examples of this kind in the next section.

Minoan branding and academia

So far, we have seen several instances of the discursive practice of branding in the commercial and community domains. These are characterised by the combination of images and texts to create shorthand logos; the construction of consistent identities; and the encouragement of brand loyalty through psychological and emotional engagement. We will now consider examples of branding within the academic discipline of Minoan archaeology, where we believe that the aforementioned processes may also be observed. A key concern will be to demonstrate how the discipline *structures* knowledge, but in the process also comes to be *structured*.

Within the academic domain perhaps the most obvious example of academic branding is the marketing of courses in Aegean/Minoan archaeology (Fairclough 1995). Prestigious universities operate as well established brands. Brochures and prospectuses usually carry the logo of the institution. The promotional literature may also contain certain phrases (or 'tag lines', to use a term from the field of advertising) which serve to reinforce the identity of the institution and/or the course and to distinguish it from its rivals.

Similar awareness of brand image is displayed by the various national Archaeological Schools, which engage in specific traditions of research; obtain funding from specific sources; and 'copyright' specific archaeological sites in which they have made long term investments. They promote readily identifiable visual representations of artefacts and architecture. Finally, they operate in distinct national languages, in which they produce daybooks, paperwork and publications (Joyce 2002; Simandiraki and Grimshaw in press). They thus create and maintain discourse communities which, for many fieldworkers and readers, are mutually exclusive. In short, the Archaeological Schools can be seen as different brands of the same product.

Whilst there are important differences between the processes of archaeological research and those of manufacturing and marketing, it may be useful to consider the similarities. Minoan archaeological research involves the following interconnected elements (Kardulias 1994, 378-85; Preziosi 2002; Keller 2003, fig.598; Cherry *et al.* 2005),

- the raw material (artefacts/ monuments).

- the knowledge producer (the archaeologist, who applies for a permit).
- the mediator (the excavator/ Ephorate/ Archaeological School).
- the production regulator (the Ministry).
- the investor (the funding body).
- the market (the Minoan academic community).
- the product (knowledge/ a research output).
- the packaging (publication/ exhibition).
- the distributor (the publishing house/ the exhibiting institution/ the teaching staff).

To extend this metaphor, a successful brand is one which is associated with a strong product (e.g. a research publication), which targets an appropriate market segment (i.e. a specialist readership), has a reliable distributor (i.e. publisher), and enjoys a good reputation in the market (i.e. the ranking of the publication on a scale of quality assurance).

Again, let us consider a specific product. The cover of the latest *Guide to the Archaeological Museum of Herakleion* (Fig.6) exemplifies the visual and textual construction of academic and artifactual identities. The cover depicts particular artefacts and not others. All of the artefacts on the cover could, at the time of publication, be found in the museum (which holds the world's largest collection of Minoan artefacts). The book advertises the artefacts, inviting visitors to go and see them 'in the flesh'. It therefore brands the museum. It also brands the archaeologist who authored the guidebook, as well as those who excavated the artefacts.

Publications play an integral role in the construction of the discipline of Minoan archaeology. They conform to certain textual conventions which distinguish them from those of other fields, including the presentation of diagrams, the use of acronyms and bibliographic standards. More specifically, the publishers follow a 'house style' which is evident in documents such as their 'guide to contributors'. In addition to these stylistic features, a range of other variables determines whether a piece of research is accepted for publication. For example, journals have editors with particular interests; they address particular themes; they are pitched at particular types of reader; and they sometimes have regular contributors. All of these standardising elements combine to brand both the journals and the knowledge contained within them. They create institutionalised, formulated ideoscapes.

The discursive construction of the discipline can also be usefully understood in terms of the professional socialisation of the archaeologist (Cherry *et al.* 2005). In order to become a Minoan archaeologist, one needs to be taught; to conduct fieldwork; to master methodologies; and to successfully emulate educators and their practices. The novice archaeologist is socialised into an artifactual and behavioural tradition. S/he is shaped by discourses of practice which determine how knowledge is generated, perpetuated or challenged (Bintliff 1984, 34; Hamilakis 1999; Hitchcock and Koudounaris 2002, 43, '…one is programmed very specifically into not raising questions or issues which might call into question the unassailability of a given scholar's pronouncements'). Over time the individual masters these dominant discourses and learns how to manipulate them in order to develop professional networks; to access resources; and to achieve progression within professional hierarchies. It can therefore be said that the archaeologist is positioned at the heart of the agency-structure dialectic, simultaneously being inscribed by professional-academic discourses while also 'writing him/herself into' those discourses (Hall 1997). In terms of the commercial metaphor, the

archaeologist consumes pre-existing Minoan data (e.g. knowledge of sites, artefacts, bibliographies), but also generates new data that sustains the enterprise (Holtorf 2002). The individual thus 'buys into' and co-creates the Minoan archaeology brand.

It is important to recognise that, within the structural parameters of the discipline, the scholar or practitioner of Minoan archaeology is able to exercise agency in choosing institutes, mentors, collaborations, sites, specialisations, research topics and personal behaviours (Aaker 1997; She 2000). But these choices may have important political consequences. For example, by studying at University X, a student comes to be associated with a particular research community and a particular mentor. The same applies in terms of attendance at conferences, lectures and commemorations of excavations. Through association with a particular Department of Archaeology or a particular research paradigm (i.e. discourse), the individual may find that (perhaps quite unintentionally) s/he is viewed with suspicion by members of a rival department or proponents of an opposing paradigm. In short, the archaeologist is branded through his/her professional, academic or personal affiliations (Balmer 2006, 35). These affiliations subsequently determine access to funding and to excavation projects.

The professionally established Minoan archaeologist engages in an ongoing process of image management. This is effected in several ways, through qualifications; geographical location; the type of fieldwork; the use of language in public displays of knowledge; collaborators; research topics; students; and so on. These can all be regarded as aspects of personal branding, in that the archaeologist seeks to project a consistent image.

It should also be noted that several Minoan archaeologists use the popular media in order to attract archaeological as well as public attention. This creates bridges between the academic field and the community. The publicity that such celebrity academics generate about their research may prompt public debates within and beyond the academic field; as well as generate new forms of cultural narratives. It can also serve to advertise the products of their archaeological research, thus attracting further investment. Let us take the example of a poster (not shown here, for ethical reasons) which advertises a public lecture by a famous archaeologist in which he will talk about his life achievements. The poster is a palimpsest. The archaeologist's photograph (in centre frame) co-exists with a photograph of one of his most famous finds; the logo of the Municipality; a text containing biographical information about the archaeologist; a text describing the organisers of the event (the Municipality, the Ministry of Culture and a local institute); and a text explaining when and where the lecture will take place. As with the aforementioned types of branding, the lecture involves a producer (the speaker), consumers (the audience) and vendors (the organisers). In addition, we can observe the construction of a consistent identity through visual and verbal strategies; and the promotion of products (excavations, publications) and services (the speaker's academic career). All of these elements combine to reinforce the archaeologist's personal brand. The poster also has 'cross over' value in that it simultaneously appeals to both specialist and non-specialist markets. Finally, brand loyalty is demonstrated by the audience's willingness to attend and to be seen attending the lecture.

From all of these examples we can conclude that Minoan archaeologists are at the same time brand producers, consumers and vendors. They simultaneously brand and are branded. They are both subject and object. They structure and are structured by traditions.

Concluding Thoughts and Recommendations

In this chapter, we have examined several processes by which the identity of Minoan archaeology is constructed within public and specialist domains. We have viewed these processes through the lens of discourse theory and, more specifically, that of branding. Our general conclusions are as follows.

The cases we have examined in this paper demonstrate that our knowledge of the Minoan past is produced and consumed much like other branded commodities. This branding of Minoan archaeology occurs in multiple domains, including the commercial, the societal (what we call community branding) and the academic. In terms of discursive practice, there is considerable overlap between these domains. In fact, in constructing itself as an academic discipline, Minoan archaeology employs very similar strategies to those used in the commercial domain, and increasingly so. Minoan archaeologists can be seen to construct themselves and their discipline through the production and consumption of branded texts.

We also believe that specialists and non-specialists alike would benefit from developing a critical awareness of branding as a discursive practice. This would help us to conceptualise the process of identity construction in Minoan archaeology in particular. But in a broader context it would help us to conceptualise how archaeological memory and tradition are produced and consumed. Some potential benefits of such an approach are that it may ameliorate aspects of disciplinary training; that it may help us to challenge reductive constructions of cultures; and that it may facilitate the development of counter-discourses against academic or public disenfranchisement.

Acknowledgements

We would like to thank the editors of this volume, Chrysanthi Gallou and Merkouris Georgiadis, for the opportunity to participate in it. We would also like to thank those colleagues who have provided valuable material for and feedback on the ideas presented here. However, all opinions and mistakes remain our own and do not represent our employers or colleagues.

References

Aaker, J.L., 1997, 'Dimensions of brand personality', *Journal of Marketing Research* XXXIV (August), 347-56.

Askegaard, S., 2006. 'Brands as a global iceoscape', *Brand Culture*, J.E. Schroeder, M. Salzer-Mörling (eds.), London and New York, 91-100.

Balmer, J.M.T., 2006. 'Corporate brand cultures and communities' *Brand Culture*, J.E. Schroeder, M. Salzer-Mörling (eds.), London and New York, 34-49.

Bilton, T., Bonnett, K., Jones, P., Skinner, D., Stanworth, M. and Webster, A., 1996. *Introductory Sociology*, London.

Bintliff, J.L., 1984. 'Structuralism and Myth in Minoan Studies', *Antiquity* 58, 33-8.

Brown, K.S., Hamilakis, Y., 2003. 'The cupboard of the yesterdays? Critical perspectives on the usable past', *The Usable Past, Greek Metahistories*, Y. Hamilakis (ed.), London, 1–19.

Burr, V., 1995. *An Introduction to Social Constructionism*, London.

Cadogan, G., 2004. ''The Minoan distance', the impact of Knossos upon the twentieth century', *Knossos, Palace, City, State*, G. Cadogan, E. Hatzaki and A.Vasilakis (eds), [British School at Athens Studies 12], London, 537-45.

Cherry, J.F., Margomenou, D. and Talalay, L (eds.), 2005. *Prehistorians Round the Pond, Reflections on Aegean Prehistory as a Discipline*, [Kelsey Museum Publication 2], Michigan.

Edgeworth, M. (ed.), 2006. *Ethnographies of Archaeological Practice, Cultural encounters, material transformations*, [Worlds of Archaeology Series], Oxford.

Fairclough, N., 1989. *Language and Power*, London.

Fairclough, N., 1992. *Discourse and Social Change*, Cambridge.

Fairclough, N., 1995. *Critical Discourse Analysis, The Critical Study of Language*, Harlow.

Hall, S., 1997. 'The work of representation', *Representation, Cultural Representations and Signifying Practices*, S. Hall (ed.), London, 15–74.

Hamilakis, Y., 1999. 'La trahison des arche´ologues? Archaeological practice as intellectual activity in postmodernity', *Journal of Mediterranean Archaeology* 12.1, 60–79.

Hamilakis, Y., 2002. 'What future for the 'Minoan' past?', *Labyrinth Revisited, Rethinking 'Minoan' Archaeology*, Y. Hamilakis (ed.), Oxford, 2–28.

Hamilakis, Y., 2006. 'The colonial, the national, and the local, legacies of the 'Minoan' past', *Archaeology and European Modernity, producing and Consuming the Minoans*, Y. Hamilakis and N. Momigliano (eds.), [Creta Antica 7], Padova, 145-62.

Hitchcock, L. and Koudounaris, P., 2002. 'Virtual Discourse, Arthur Evans and the Reconstructions of the Minoan Palace at Knossos', *Labyrinth Revisited, Rethinking 'Minoan' Archaeology*, Y. Hamilakis (ed.), Oxford, 40–58.

Holtorf, C., 2002. 'Notes on the Life History of a Pot Sherd', *Journal of Material Culture* 7.1, 49-71.

Holtorf, C., 2007. *Archaeology is a Brand! The Meaning of Archaeology in*

Contemporary Popular Culture, illustrated by Q. Drew, Oxford.

Joyce, R.A., 2002. 'The Languages of Archaeology', Social Archaeology series, Oxford.

Kardulias, P.N., 1994. 'Archaeology in modern Greece, bureaucracy, politics and science', *Beyond the Site, regional studies in the Aegean area*, P.N. Kardulias (ed.), Lanham MD, 373-85.

Keller, K.L., 2003. 'Brand Synthesis, the multidimensionality of brand knowledge', *Journal of Consumer Research* 29 (March), 595-600.

Oxford English Dictionary 2007, Oxford.

Papadopoulos, J.K., 2005. 'Inventing the Minoans, Archaeology, Modernity and the Quest for European Identity', *Journal of Mediterranean Archaeology* 18.1, 87-149.

Pennycook, A., 1994. 'Incommensurable Discourses?', *Applied Linguistics* 15.2, 115-38.

Preziosi, D., 2002. 'Archaeology as Museology, Re-thinking the Minoan Past', *Labyrinth Revisited, Rethinking 'Minoan' Archaeology*, Y. Hamilakis (ed.), Oxford, 30-9.

Schroeder, J.E and Salzer-Mörling, M. (eds.) 2006. *Brand Culture*, London and New York.

She, 2000. 'Sex and a Career', *World Archaeology* 32.2, 166-72.

Simandiraki, A., 2004. 'Μινωπαιδιές, the Minoan Civilisation in Greek Primary Education', *World Archaeology* 36.2, 177-88.

Simandiraki, A., 2005. 'Minoan archaeology in the Athens 2004 Olympic Games', *European Journal of Archaeology* 8.2, 157-81.

Simandiraki, A., 2006. 'The 'Minoan' experience of schoolchildren in Crete', *Archaeology and European Modernity, producing and Consuming the Minoans*, Y. Hamilakis, N. Momigliano (eds.), [Creta Antica 7], Padova, 259-74.

Simandiraki, A., (in press). 'Minoan archaeology in modern Cretan administration', *Proceedings of the 10th International Congress of Cretan Studies*, Chania

Simandiraki, A., Grimshaw, T., (in press). 'Linguistic Imperialism and Minoan Archaeology', *Archaeologies*.

Solomon, E., 2003. 'Constructing local identity through archaeological finds, The case of Knossos (Crete, Greece)', *Museological Review* 10 (Special Issue), 31-47.

Solomon, E., 2005. 'Το αρχαιολογικό μνημείο ως τοπίο, ανθρωπολογικές προσεγγίσεις μίας γεωγραφικής έννοιας', *Κριτική Διεπιστημονικότητα, Διεπιστημονικότητα, Πολιτισμικές Αντιστάσεις* 1, 74-82.

Solomon E., 2006a. 'Προς μία ανθρωπολογική προσέγγιση της Κνωσού, ζητήματα σύγχρονης κρητικής ταυτότητας και μινωική κληρονομιά', *Proceedings of the 9th International Cretological Congress*, vol. A3, A4, Herakleion, 33-49.

Solomon E., 2006b. 'Knossos, Social Uses of a Monumental Landscape', *Archaeology and European Modernity, producing and Consuming the Minoans*, Y. Hamilakis, N. Momigliano (eds.), [Creta Antica 7], Padova, 163-82.

Usher, R., Edwards, R., 1994. *Postmodernism and Education*, London.

Vasilakos, A., no date. *Αρχαιολογικό Μουσείο Ηρακλείου, Οδηγός του Επισκέπτη*, Athens.

Wodak, R., de Cillia, R., Reisigl, M., Liebhart, K., 1999. *The Discursive Construction of National Identity*, translated by A. Hirsch and R. Mitten, Edinburgh.

Figure 1. An example of Minoan archaeology commercial branding, a Knossos wine (photos by the authors).

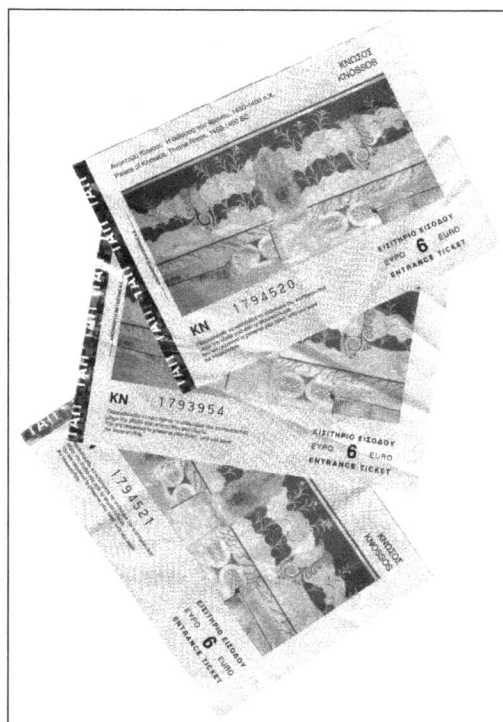

Figure 2. An example of Minoan archaeology commercial branding, Knossos Palace tickets, (photos by the authors).

Figure 3. An example of Minoan archaeology community branding, the Herakleion Prefecture tourist booklet, August 2006 (photo by Simandiraki).

Figure 4. An example of Minoan archaeology community branding, cabinet in the office of the Chania Prefect (photo by Simandiraki).

Figure 5. An example of Minoan archaeology community branding,
Yianna Daskalaki-Angelopoulou (chief public face of the Athens 2004 Olympic Games)
lighting the Olympic Flame in front of Evans's reconstruction of the North Propylon of the
Knossos Palace, July 2004 (after 'Maris News' magazine 8 (2005), 26).

Figure 6. The cover of the latest (now obsolete) official guidebook to the Herakleion Museum (after Vasilakis, no date).

Material Identity – Archaeology and National Identity

Charlotta Hillerdal

Introduction

Our modern world is organised into a multitude of sovereign nation-states. A nation is perceived as the natural state of community. The common ground among the people of a nation is, except for politics, laws and regulations, a sense of shared traditions and values; partly originating from a common history. There is a collective and unifying force in the idea of shared experiences, and the further back these experiences originate, the stronger the sense of authentic communality. A nation is as strong as its people, and a people are as strong as its history.

This world of nations is the basic preconception of our time. Since childhood we are formed in moulds shaped by the nation. We are brought up to belong to the culture of our nation, to embrace the national values and to feel solidarity with the others sharing these values. This has the consequence that the national description of history controls our vision of the past.

Professional archaeologists, who construct the 'official prehistory', without being particularly nationalistic, still participate in the national discourse about the past. The identity constructing function of archaeology remains as important now as it was in the national romantic era of the 19th century, if only less visible. This can easily be seen in the discussions concerning cultural heritage and preservation.

The story of the past

The past and history are not the same; but the past is the object of history. History is the story of the past told to the present; it is our representation of what has been.

The past is not autonomous, but dependent on the present to tell its story; it can only be reached through the mediation of history. This makes the story of the past dependent on the present. History, therefore, is created in a contemporary context, and serves the needs of contemporaneity. History, however, need not be told for the sake of the past.

History is often referred to as a dialogue between past and present (Selberg 2002, 12). It might be closer to the truth to describe this communication as a monologue. The past and the present have a one-sided relationship; the past, or at least history, is an actor in the present, but the past takes no interest in the present.

History is the story in retrospect, where the outcome is already clear and the future is near at hand. The historic narrative is always presenting one, or more, aspects of the past seen from the perspective of the present. It is always contradictory, simplified, exaggerated and restrained, and often one-dimensional and static. As a result it can also be outdated and old-fashioned. The past, on the other hand, can never be, or rather always is, outdated.

History is part of the description of society, and serves a purpose in society other than describing the past. History, tradition and identity are concepts intimately connected to each other. One of the cornerstones in a modern community therefore is its common history, and one of the most important functions of history is to create community. History and community are dependent on each other, and when that community is a nation, the history is unavoidably a national history.

National history is the commonly agreed upon story of the past; the official version, one could say. It lays the foundation of rational communality, and often strives to let the national entity stretch far into prehistory. This view of the past is however anachronistic; it presupposes - and creates - a unity that was never there. History and archaeology of today is usually created within the national narrative, i.e. the established, neutralised and naturalised story about the nation state.

Our concept of history is contemporary with the modern society; a child of enlightenment and romanticism. During the 19th century history became professionalized as a science. Thoughts of evolution and progress put their marks on the concept of history in the form of a linear history, where society evolves from one state of being to the next. With that follow the idea of a beginning and an end, and also the implication of today as history's destination (Eriksen 1996, 40-1). The nation-state, also a part of modern philosophy; is intimately connected to history. In this ideology the nation became the result of the historic development; the end product of historic progress (Eriksen 1996, 42).
History is not only an academic subject, but functions as an active participant in society. The contemporary analysis of the present always includes an aspect of pastness; the past becomes the explanation of the present. History support society with substance; historical continuity validates and strengthens a society's claim to authenticity.

History builds identity; in fact one can hardly imagine a definition of identity lacking the concept of history, or a past; be it personal, local or national. From that aspect, history not only provides authenticity, but also confidence.

This 'unifying' function of history is perceived as a positive, and almost necessary, force in society. In fact, the history-less society is often pictured as an ignorant and dangerous society. Historic knowledge is close to an obligation; the heritage, our heritage, has to be preserved, and transferred, to the future. If we ignore to do that, we rob our children of their past, and consequently their anchorage to history, their roots and ultimately their identity.

There is a schism between professional - or academic - history and popular history that results in two very different stories being told. Professional historians, and archaeologists, are the producers of historical knowledge, and cannot frame themselves from the role played by history in society. We have to take responsibility for our truths. Few professional archaeologists would admit to participating in the national narrative, but as long as the opposition is a 'silent knowledge' conducted within the framework of an established historical truth, national history will prevail.

A nation and its people

A nation draws history behind it, like the wake of a great ship (Chapman *et al.* 1989, 7).

According to the archaeologist Kristiensen (1993, 12), 'History has become the dominant ideology of the present'. This is not a new trend, but can be seen as a consequence of the modern nation state.

One of the most influential modern theories on nations and nationalism is Anderson's *Imagined Communities* (1991). To Anderson

(1991) a nation is an imagined community kept together by the idea of communality. This form of community can only emerge when a ruler or king no longer has divine and absolute power, when the printed word can be spread and read by a large number of people, and when there is a bourgeoisie (Anderson 1991, 36). These conditions were only fulfilled after the enlightenment and bourgeoisie revolutions of the late 18th century. The nation state therefore is a modern construction.

When king or God no longer defines the general structure; unity has to be found elsewhere. Collective unity was perceived to be imbedded in the language and traditions of people. The nation was understood as a culturally constituted natural unit (Eriksen 1996, 74). Part of the national construction is formed on the idea of a common past. 'If nation-states are widely conceded to be 'new' and 'historical', the nations to which they give political expression always loom out of an immemorial past, and, still more important, glide into a limitless future' (Anderson 1991, 11-2). The idea of a national history is therefore essential to the structure.

Nationalistic ideology and national history were not thoughts new for the modern era, but can for example be found in the rhetoric of the Great Power Sweden in the 17th century. The nationalism of the 19th century however, differs from previous times in that it aims towards including the citizens in the national paradigm; and the people in history. The modern understanding of states raised objections to the idea of sovereignty of king and state, and legitimacy in power had to be found somewhere else. This was established in the people of the state, the people, understood as the natural unit that formed the nations.

It is nature which educates families: the most natural state is, therefore, one nation, an extended family with one national character. This it retains for

ages and develops most naturally if the leaders come from the people and are wholly dedicated to it. For a nation is as natural a plant as a family, only with more branches (Herder 1969, 324).

The modern formulation of states is characterised by ideas of people and culture developed by the German philosopher Herder in the late 18th century. According to Herder (1969) nations are upheld by the people. History is a whole, it is a chain formed by processes of socialisation and tradition. 'No one lives in his own period only; he builds on what has gone before and lays a foundation for what comes after' (Herder 1969, 188). Knowledge is transmitted from one generation to the next by imitation and exercise; this transmission is called tradition, and the process and understanding of this tradition is culture (Herder 1969, 313). The possession of a common culture creates the folk, or nation. 'The natural state of man is society' (Herder 1969, 317), and communality is created by tradition. History, by this reasoning has a central place in the creation of society, and the true community is that with common traditions and in the extension common origin.

The idea of folk and culture became central in the national ideology. Nations was to be formed around the idea of a people of common traditions and interests, constituting the core of the national spirit; folk culture was singled out as the superior national culture (Eriksen 1993, 18-9). Folk culture was perceived as timeless (Schousboe 1989, 166), and a contrast to the loss of originality displayed by the industrialised parts of society (Abrahams 2000, 16).

Consequently, 19th century academia turned its attention to the farmer population. Intellectuals went out into rural areas to collect and record traditional customs and costumes of the country people, folklore was established as a concept, and national museums were created displaying this traditional culture. The philosophy behind this interest was the notion that these groups in society had long preserved traditions, reminiscences of ancient times (Alver 1980, 5-7). The ethnographic research aimed towards restoring the authentic history of the nation and its people; and to create a collective subject for history (Anshelm 1993, 11). This new interest in traditional culture can therefore be related to the idea of a national (pre-) historic past; where the traditional life served as a rediscovered link to this past.

In the discovery of folk culture and in elevating it to become national culture, folk culture was created (Eriksen 1993, 20). Culture was made essential - naturalised into the definition of people hood. One united people should equal one shared homogenous culture (Mathisen 2000, 179). A homogenization process took place, where certain cultural traits were understood as part of the 'national spirit'. More locally formed identities where to be forged into a common sense of national identity. It was the task of the nation to make the boundaries of ethnic groups matching the boundaries of the state. National identity can be said to be the officially chosen and implied ethnic identity.

In the same process the common became the norm, in an idealized form. Courtiers were portrayed in folk costumes, and customs collected from the countryside traveled into the bourgeoisie and upper-class homes of the cities.

> The discipline of folklore carves out a special place in the bourgeois economic and cultural dynamic. For the 'folk' were a construct of the developing nation-states, often as a counterpoint to the banalities of life within a commercializing society. The 'folk' under these conditions emerged full-blown as a conglomerate term for those peoples who maintain a sense of connectedness to the past, and especially 'the land' (Abrahams 2000, 16).

As well as the folk being a link to the past, it was a curiosity and something almost exotic, untouched and naive, and it was these qualities that had preserved the traditions through generations. The folksongs and folk sagas had no problem expressing the prehistoric past, since the folk were not problemised according to evolutionary theories of progress, but had conserved the past in a parallel side-track.

The ideology of national culture as a consequence of history creates an essentialist perspective on people and identity. To the core of this way of thinking lies the idea of authenticity; preserved originality transmitted through generations linking person to person and past to present in a natural state of communality. Now can be explained by then, and we through them. This view of the past has lingered in historical analysis and influenced later theories of people and ethnicity.

Most nations present their history as a natural necessity. The homogenization of the nation is, as history, experienced as linear and finished process (Aronsson 2006, 25). The homogenization process of Sweden must be described as a success. There is a common preconception that the Swedish state rests on a pure ethno-national foundation; with a homogenous population, that had little involvement with outsiders, and a continuity traceable back to the time when the inland ice melted (Grundberg 2004, 24-5), and, as one of the oldest nations in Europe, having numerous memories from the past (Rosenberg 2006, 17). Multicultural and multiethnic states are described as a new condition for previously homogenous nations to handle (Anttonen 1996, 8). This is rather a result of a successful national ideology, than a reflection of true events.

A nation and its prehistory

Archaeology evolved as an academic subject in the 19th century; the same time that grew the modern conception of the nation. It was a time that the defined the core of nationhood; searched for a national identity and evoke the idea of a national spirit. Archaeology participated in this mission by providing the nation with deeply growing roots of ancient history; tracing the traditions of the people back through the ages. Archaeology is therefore to its very constitution a national matter.

The notion of cultural continuity and historical authenticity contribute to the idea of an essential material history. The archaeological material is in its physicality a very powerful symbol of the past. Material objects are easily turned into representations of authentic culture (Mathisen 2000, 187). The presence of the remains is an unquestionable argument to the presence of the past, and actualises concepts of heredity, continuity and authenticity. The material remains represent the pre-historic origin and becomes proof of the past.

Archaeological practice is to its character place bound. One discovers the very physical remains of an event, person or concept, all bound to a physical place, be it a farm, a village, a shire or a country. From this aspect the archaeological material also gives a strong argument to the nation.

Archaeological remains have often been used as national symbols. In Sweden the grave mounds and surrounding landscape of Old Uppsala (Fig.1) has become the iconic symbol of Sweden's past. This location has been designated the cradle of the Swedish realm already in the 17th century (Wallette 2004, 127), and are given profound significance, in scientific discussions as well as in popular contexts.

The national narrative is the unspoken presupposition of most archaeological practice; and most stories created by archaeologists fall within the frames of this narrative. The tradition of the official national history is hard to break; it reproduces itself through scientific as well as popular history and archaeology; following the same established outlines. When not contested the idea of nations and nationality is projected back through time into prehistory. In terminology such as *Swedish Stone Age* and *Swedish Vikings* the national paradigm is upheld, told and transmitted into the future.

In cases of minority groups, 'new'- or politically unstable states the ethnic- or nationalistic aspect of archaeology is obvious, and can sometimes even be found on the agenda. This type of archaeological practice instantly become controversial, and archaeologist working in these conditions are often criticised as being bias or unscientific by the archaeological community in recognised states. This is sometimes justified, but in many cases it is only a question of an uncertain political situation being reflected into archaeological practice.

One often meets with the condescending attitude that this nationalistic historical analysis is a phase all nations need to go through. Behind this statement lies the rather smug conclusion that we, the old nations, have passed and overcome this naive time in historical development, and advanced onto a critical and nuanced view of our past. This is in the same time an admittance that our nation already passed through that stage, and moved on. The question is; moved on to what?

The next step in a nation's history-construction occurs when the nationalistic statements have become neutralised and commonly accepted as national history. The historical statements need no longer be extreme when they belong to an established narrative. The fact is that we are dealing with different phases of the same phenomena; the phase of construction and the phase of maintenance. The activist propaganda on the barricades calms down to take the shape of a prosaic backdrop. However, even when working from the stage with the prosaic backdrop, a nationalistic outlook pervades historical and archaeological discourse.

Archaeology is, therefore, to some extent, a subject of the nation. A reformulation of archaeology would crave a reformation of the national narrative, and with that a new goal for historic knowledge.

A nation and its heritage

> We are not necessarily a conservative and nostalgic company. We can both offer and deny legitimacy to a social and cultural policy that asks for a historical perspective for the present (Grundberg 1998, 47).

Cultural heritage is the ultimate product of the politically correct history. It is a dated, and possibly outdated, idea associated with the emerging nation state. Cultural heritage has been explained as collective memory (Sörbom 1998, 5; Grundberg 2002, 13), as 'materialised images of collective ideas and values' (Jensen 1998, 99), as manifestations of human culture (Biörnstad 1997, 37), as a collection of myths about a group, their territory and their history (Molin 2003, 22), or as 'the materialised and collective soul of the nation' (Jensen 1998, 104). The term cultural heritage came into use in the 19th century; and was an expression of the attempt to create a national identity, strengthen the inner solidarity and give the state status among other states (Horgby and Lindström 2002, 309-10). What is clear in all definitions is that heritage is a question concerning group solidarity and collectivity. Cultural heritage is the progressive use of history expressed in society (Grundberg 2004, 10). It is a concept in and for society, and can not be relevant outside the context of society.

Cultural heritage is the material expression of the official history; it is the chosen collective memory displaying what we want to remember from the past. It is always a matter of ideology and politics; not everything can be preserved; some traces from the past prove to be more valuable than others and are promoted to cultural heritage. This choice has to be made by someone; and consequently the state officials are given a preferential right to interpretation. Cultural heritage is created in an ongoing process where people materialise memory into culture. Defined as a collective memory is also becomes a legitimation of memories; and an expression of the 'correct' history (Grundberg 2002, 13-4). This correct history; reproduced and reformulated, is a contemporary conception, and its material manifestation, heritage, is a contemporary construction; it is a reflection of our present selves in the mirror glass of the past.

However, cultural heritage builds on voluntary communality, and can only be of importance as long as it holds relevance for the citizens. The cultural heritage has to be experienced as something that concerns you; which means keeping the heritage modern, in the sense of being adapted to society (Strömholm 1997, 13-4; Hauan 2002, 142). In Sweden today it is not possible to base a Swedish identity on the heritage of an ethnically homogenous group. Cultural heritage can on the other hand be used to create understanding between people, and be reformulated to work as a platform for integration. The insight in heritage politics that there are not one but many heritages has vitalised the concept somewhat (Grundberg 1998, 43; Biörnstad 1997, 43).

The idea of a cultural heritage still comprises the 19th century's aspiration towards the authentic, nationally primordial, unspoiled cultural elements. The original nationalistic thought on heritage was to incorporate certain elements into national history as an expression for the folk soul; culture became almost equal to people. Parts of the cultural heritage, museums and monuments, are a historical heritage from this cultural process in the 19th - and early 20th centuries. Museums and other preserving institutions pick stereotypes to represent the themes central to the national construction (Grundberg 1998, 316; 2002, 17-8; Horgby and Lindström 2002, 313-5). The cultural heritage then is both historic and static, and contemporary and political. Static because when something has been designated cultural heritage it will be preserved as that. It is therefore a result of how previous generations made use of history and an active ongoing process of selection and writing history in the presence (Grundberg 2004, 12).

The principle behind cultural heritage is to distinguish and preserve. It is a concept aiming towards the future, in that the object already exists in the present, but need to be preserved for the future. One aspect of the cultural heritage is conservationist and conservative.

As a political concept cultural heritage is central, and even manifested as a human right. It is often mentioned in terms of cultural rescore and is said to be a basic and uniting medium is society (Biörnstad 1997, 371; Strömholm 1997, 14). Its preservation and maintenance is motivated as being beneficial for society and its citizens (Anshelm 1993, 17). It is perceives to be a rescore for knowledge and identity construction (Hauan 2002, 141).

In the last decade, immigration and political instability in the surrounding world has called into question the idea of a homogeneous cultural heritage and its connection to the nation. From professionals within the heritage sector it has been noticed that there is a responsibility connected to creating foundations for identity, and attention has been drawn to the importance of presenting manifold, liberal and differentiated stories and perspectives (Lindvall 2002, 8-16). In Sweden there has also been a political direction to adapt the cultural heritage to the multicultural society

(Beckman 2002, 52). Heritage, it is claimed, can instead be used as an argument for local, different and disparate identities (Johansen 2002, 44; Grundberg 2004, 75). This is not necessarily the way of making heritage valid for all. Attempts to make the heritage multicultural, to better fit contemporary society, is only another way of presenting an essentialist cultural history. The purpose of showing ethnic and cultural multiplicity in heritage, presupposes background and ancestry as something important. This, according to the archaeologist Anders Högberg, might confirm differences rather than to create unity (Högberg 2006, 81). In the end, cultural heritage is still described through identity and confirmation, even though 'national' is exchanged for 'local' or 'mixed'.

The Swedish historians Horgby and Lindström (2002) state the opinion that cultural heritage, if considered to be created in a dialogue between the present and the past, can have a more dynamic character than given to it by the idea of collective memory. That, they mean, could turn heritage into a scientifically workable concept (Horgby and Lindström 2002, 320). Heritage can not manage this flexibility; it has to simplify history, and it must represent something. Where history can manage being problemised, and even gain credibility from it, heritage can only be one dimensional. The whole concept of cultural heritage demands an idea of an identity based in the past; without this thought the whole construction falls. As a scientific concept therefore, cultural heritage has little value. The problem is that as a political concept it has great relevance for society, and that what is perceived as cultural heritage is the direct and visible result of archaeology. This creates a paradoxical situation of mutual dependency, where a concept without scientific relevance has to be kept alive in the academic discourse.

Sweden and its Vikings

Every nation has its historical icons. In Sweden it is the Vikings that are the prime contributors to the national self-esteem. The Viking is an amorphous figure that succeeds in representing a wide range of different characteristics said to be connected to the Swedish 'folk-spirit'; masculinity, the crude but noble warrior, the courageous explorer, the free land owner, the independent woman. He even manages to represent democratic values.

The Viking was chosen as a national hero already in the 19th century, and several very popular literate works spread this notion. One of the most influential was *Frithiofs saga* by Tegnér, published in whole for the first time in 1825, which for several decades was among the obligatory literature read by Swedish school children.

Tegnér was a member of 'Götiska förbundet' (Geatish Association), which was formed in 1311, originally as a jaunty society with literary aspirations where the members took names of Old Norse mythology. Moreover, it had a patriotic cause as well, emphasizing the Old Norse culture with the aim of being politic and educational (Grandien 1987, 45-6).

The Geatish idea stemmed from the notion that the Swedes were the descendants of the Goths, who once defeated Rome (Rehnberg 1980, 17). These thoughts had been elaborated in 17th century Sweden, to provide the at that time great political power of Sweden with as glorious a past as possible (Grandien 1987, 27). Prehistory, and its remains, became 'political alibis', to use the words of Årre (1998, 130), for the Great Power Sweden. The ancient monuments served a propagandistic value for the Swedish state. In 1666, Sweden got its first law protecting ancient remains, which makes it the oldest in the world (Jensen 1997, 135). The idea of revering the past has therefore been founded in Swedish legislation for several hundred years.

The Old Norse society as the root of the Swedish realm was first noticed by 17th century academic Olof Rudbeck in his historical work *Atlantica*. He was the first to use Norse literature as source for national history. Rudbeck proved most of European culture and history to originate from Sweden; and that the character of the Norse, their wisdom and their fearlessness in battle, and their support for king and state still comprised the foundation for the Swedish realm. Rudbecks use of the Norse literature was however a genealogical one, aiming towards creating the chronicles of king, state and royal family (Walette 2004, 44, 59, 161-3).

In early 19th century Sweden, as well as in the rest of Europe, the people as a concept is found more and more in foci of politics and philosophy. The power of the Swedish king was weakened to the benefit of the citizens, and nationalistic feelings were strengthened by the loss of Finland to Russia in the war of 1809. It is recognised that there in Sweden exists unique qualities that should be shared and defended by all. The concept of folk emerges in 1784, with the *folk saga*, and in 1817 the traditional clothing of the peasants is given the name *folk costume* (Stenroth 2005, 10-25). In 1828 the law of protection of ancient remains was reformulated from protection of the 'manly accomplishments of Sweden's and Götaland's kings' to the 'preservation of the memories of the inhabitants of the fatherland' (Grundberg 2004, 13, my translation). It is a good example on how the mentality concerning the past in the 19th century shifted focus from king to folk, and also from admiration to ancestry. History has become the concern of everyone.

One central member of 'Götiska förbundet', as well as the editor of its periodical *Iduna*, was historian and romantic lyricist Geijer. Geijer was of the opinion that the people carry history, for Geijer Sweden was the Swedish people. To the contrast of the 17th century idea as sources on genealogy of the kings, the Norse sagas and mythology was given a new function as folk-poetry, and means of knowledge of the Norse mentality. In Norse society the peasant was the equal of the king; the freeborn landowners, poor next to wealthy, comprised the true nation (Wallette 2004, 227-63). Geijer's two historical works *Svea rikes häfder* (1825) and *Svenska folkets historia* (first part published in 1832) had an important impact on Swedish historical research (Wallette 2004, 45), but it is foremost through his poetry that Geijer is remembered. Many of his poems portray Norse society, and have contributed to the national romantic idea of the Viking Age.

'Götiska förbundet' explored ancient remains and folklore as well as literature. In the spirit of the time, archaeology and ethnology was perceived as parts of the same genre. The real goal for the research in ethnology and folklore was the Old Norse society, and reconnecting with the virtues of Old (Grandien 1987, 66). The first collection of Swedish folk songs, collected by vicar Afzelius, who distinguished himself as a folklorist and also translated Icelandic sagas into Swedish, and Geijer, both members of Götiska förbundet, was published in 1814-17 (Rehnberg 1980, 26).

'Götiska Förbundet' was active some twenty years, and was finally disbanded in 1844. During the realistic era of the 1830s the romantic pre-history advocated by the association was criticised; but the national romanticism had got its hold over pre-history (Grandien 1987, 62). The Viking has continued to be a popular literary figure, kept alive through characters like Röde Orm of the Long Ships and Hägar the Horrible.

Despite modern archaeological research, and the fact than the historical museum in Stockholm on their home page state that the Vikings was not a people in a modern sense,

and that Sweden did not exist during the era of the Vikings (http://www.historiska.se/historia/jarnaldern/vikingar/begreppetvikingar/), the Viking resists any attempt to excommunicate him. The popular Swedish Viking is made up of a mix of archaeological science, historical prejudices, national romanticism and plain popular constructions. Principally he is a representation of the Swedish; and as well as we carry the virtues of he Vikings, the Viking carry the virtues of us. The Viking and his attributes are one of the most common national symbols in Sweden, found at any tourist store or airport, but also symbolising Sweden on liquor bottles, by the hockey league and in soccer games. It is the foremost national symbol of the past, based on tradition, continuity and roots.

It might also be worth noticing that there is a 'mini-imperialistic' thought in the Swedish treatment of the Viking Age. The iconic type of Viking ship found in Gokstad and Oseberg in Norway, constantly used in different nationalistic representations, and often clad in the Swedish colours of blue and yellow, have never been found within the geographic borders of Sweden. Nor can the Swedes take much credit for the establishments of colonies in England and Iceland, or in the pre-Columbian settling of America. This too is a legacy from the 19th century, when the Nordic countries and the people of Scandinavia, from the Swedish perspective, constituted the common foundation of political and folk community. In Norway, where the constitution of the people also coincided with struggle for autonomy, this 'Scandinavianism' was not as strong (Grandien 1987, 23-6).

At the Heritage Days in Edmonton, Canada 2006

Canada represents a society with totally different views on ethnicity than the European states, in a truly multicultural society that manages to recognise cultural differences but still presents a clear national identity. At the Heritage Days of Edmonton, the different inhabitant groups of the city present their cultural roots through folk dances, traditional food and costumes. Walking from one colourful stereotype to the next, I find myself outside the Scandinavian pavilion, clearly marked by a model of a Viking ship (Fig.2). Some traditional Scandinavian dishes are served by ladies wearing 'Scandinavian' costumes, a modified version of the Viking age dress. Alfred Nobel and Swedish Match are hidden away in the far corner of the pavilion, and novelties like Eriksson or the modern music industry is nowhere to be seen. Scandinavian culture is without doubt its Vikings; the cultural essence of Scandinavia is a 200-year old historic stereotype representing a 1000-year old culture.

At the closed coastal regiment in Vaxholm, Sweden 2007

In among the hoses, facing the sea, at the now closed regiment KA1 on the island Rindö in the Swedish archipelago stands a monument in memory of the soldiers once serving here. It has the shape and stylistic design of a Viking Age rune stone, decorated with a Viking ship (Fig.3). The runic inscription read; 'Krigarskaran (Kustjägarna) lät resa denna sten till minne efter sina gamla kämpar. Icke skall ett minnesmärke vara förmer än detta över stridbara män'.[1] This memorial was donated by the association of coastal rangers' veterans in association to the 100-years celebration of the Swedish Coastal Rangers in 2002. In this abandoned military harbour, now slowly turning into a marina, surrounded by rather mundane barracks we are supposed to stop and contemplate the bravery of the Swedish military force, as strong and masculine as ever the Vikings.

---

[1] The troop of warriors (coastal rangers) had this stone erected to commemorate their old warriors. No monument should be more than this over men with fighting sprit.

Conclusions

Nations has been the base for interpretations of common identities since the late 18th century. This 'geographical coincidence' (Gaunt and Löfgren 1984, 124) has created the framework for historic and pre-historic communality and the concept of folk and cultural roots. Notions like origin, ancestry and authenticity has characterised national history and its relation to archaeological remains. History is given an essential cultural core. 'The general talk on cultural roots has also created a great deal of unreflexive history, as it tends to naturalize (…) a particular construction of history' (Anttonen 1996, 22).

The homogenisation process of nations has created a sense of an uncomplicated relation to the past as our past, our roots and our origin. Anttonen speaks about 'the 'hidden' history of heterogeneity in the homogenous nation-state' (Anttonen 2000, 175), referring to minority groups. This could however be described as comprising the nation on a whole; a united people crave a common culture, therefore divinations, discontinuities, breaks with tradition etc. do not become part of history.

According to Grundberg (2004, 48), all collective communities are false, since they are constructions. This too is a bad argument against essentialist history writing. Cultural communities are not false because they are created; they are as real as any social constructions, they are however constructions, and as such provides no firm foundation for historical explanations of common culture. Science has to come to a realisation that culture, as well as cultural heritage, is something created in the here and now, and that the past is never enough to build a community on. It is created from influences from all over the world, and all over the time, and sometimes it is founded in fantasies. This of course does not make it unreal, or non-existent, but it does make it an unstable foundation for authenticity arguments, base for legitimacy claims, historical truths or a starting point for fighting a war against difference. Nor can it be used to create firm borders towards the other.

The presence of the past is undisputable when it comes to material remains, and in their mere existence they give argument to different historical constructions of continuity and authenticity. The archaeological material becomes a symbol far beyond the archaeological interpretations. I would like to see a new attitude in historic science, where history and archaeology as well as their material traces, are given another value, and are not assessed from the point of identity.

References

Abrahams, R.D., 2000. 'Narratives of Location and Dislocation', *Folklore, Heritage Politics and Ethnic Diversity. A Festschrift for Barbro Klein*, P. Anttonen (ed.), Botkyrka, 15-20.

Alver, B., 1980. 'Nasjonalisme og identitet. Folklore og nasjonal utvikling', *Folklore och Nationsbyggande I Norden*, L. Honko (ed.), Åbo, 5-16.

Anderson, B., 1991. *Imagined Communities. Reflections on the Origin and Spread of Nationalism. Revised Edition*, London.

Anselm, J., 1993. 'Inledning', *Modernisering och kulturarv*, J. Anselm (ed.), Stockholm, 9-22.

Anttonen, P.J., 1996. 'Introduction: Tradition and Political Identity', *Making Europe in Nordic Contexts*, P.J. Anttonen (ed.), Turku, 7-40.

Anttonen, P. J., 2000. 'Cultural Homogeneity and the National Unification of a Political Community', *Folklore, Heritage Politics and Ethnic Diversity. A Festschrift for Barbro Klein*, P.J. Anttonen (ed.), Botkyrka, 253-78.

Aronsson, P., 2006. 'Bortom den stora berättelsen. Arkeologi och historia i en mångkulturell värld', *Arkeologi och mångkultur. Rapport från Svenskt arkeologmöte 2006*, M. Burström (ed.), Södertörns högskola, 23-34.

Beckman, S., 2002. 'Kulturarvens framtider. En personlig betraktelse', *Inspiration Diskussion. Agenda Kulturarv*, K. Lindvall and B. Johansen (eds.), Stockholm, 52-65.

Biörnstad, M., 1997. 'För förståelse eller förtjänst', *Tolv kommentarer Om kulturens roll och roller. Kommentarer i anledning av en världskommissions rapport*, B. Göransson (ed.), Stockholm, 37-44.

Chapman, M., Mc Donald M. and Tonkin E., 1989. 'Introduction', *History and Ethnicity*, M. Chapman, M. McDonald and E. Tonkin (ed.), London, 1-21.

Eriksen, A., 1993. 'Den nasjonale kulturarven - en del av det moderne', *Kulturella perspektiv. Svensk etnologisk tidskrift* 1, 16-25.

Eriksen, A., 1996. 'Vi må kjenne våre røtter. Historien og modernitetens mytologi', *Myte i møte med det moderne*, L. Mikaelsson (ed.), Oslo, 32-46.

Eriksen, T.H., 1996. 'Opplysning og romantikk. Nittitalets håndtering av kulturbegrepet', *Norsk Antropologisk Tidsskrift* 2, 73-8.

Gaunt, D. and Löfgren, O., 1984. *Myter om svensken*, Stockholm.

Grandien, B., 1987. *Rönndruvans glöd. Nygöticistiskt i tanke, konst och miljö under 1800-talet*, Stockholm.

Grundberg, J., 1998. 'Archaeological Heritage Management in a Critical Perspective', *The Kaleidoscopic Past*, A. Anderson, Å. Gillberg, O.W. Jensen, H. Karlsson and M. Rolöf (eds.), Göteborg, 41-7.

Grundberg, J., 2002. *Kulturarv, turism och regional utveckling*, Östersund

Grundberg, J., 2004. *Historiebruk, globalisering och kulturarvsförvaltning. Utveckling eller konflikt?*, Göteborg.

Hauan, M., 2002. 'Fotefar mot nord. Kulturminnevernets fotfeste i folkets røtter?'

Historien in på livet, A. Eriksen, J. Garnet and T. Selberg (eds.), Lund, 127-46.

Herder, J.G., 1969. *J. G. Herder on Social and Political Culture*, Cambridge.

Horgby, B. and Lindström, D., 2002. 'Begreppet kulturarv - något för historievetenskapen?', *Historisk Tidskrift* 2, 309-22.

Högberg, A., 2006 'Kommentarer', *Arkeologi och mångkultur. Rapport från Svenskt arkeologmöte 2006*, M. Burström (ed.), Södertörns högskola, 81-4.

Jensen, O.W., 1998. 'The Cultural Heritage: Modes of Preservation and the Longing for Eternal Life', *The Kaleidoscopic Past*, A. Anderson, Å. Gillberg, O.W. Jensen, H. Karlsson and M. Rolöf (eds.), Göteborg, 99-118.

Johansen, B., 2002. 'Antikvariska dilemman. Eller meningen med kulturarv', *Inspiration Diskussion. Agenda Kulturarv*, K. Lindvall and B. Johansen (eds.), Stockholm, 37-51.

Kristiansen, K., 1993. 'The Strength of the Past and its Great Might: An essay on the use of the past', *Journal of European Archaeology* 1, 3-32.

Lindvall, K., 2002. 'Historieanvändning och politik. Mot en ny kulturarvsideologi', *Inspiration Diskussion. Agenda Kulturarv*, K. Lindvall and B. Johansen (eds.), Stockholm, 4-19.

Mathisen, S.R., 2000. 'Travels and Narratives: Itinerant Constructions of a Homogenous Sami Heritage', *Folklore, Heritage Politics and Ethnic Diversity. A Festschrift for Barbro Klein*, P.J. Anttonen (ed.), Botkyrka, 179-205.

Molin, T., 2003. *Den rätta tidens mått. Götiska förbundet, fornforskningen och det antikvariska landskapet*, Umeå.

Rehnberg, M., 1980. 'Folkloristiska inslag i olika tidevarvs idéströmningar kring det egna landet', *Folklore och Nationsbyggande I Norden*, L. Honko (ed.), Åbo, 17-32.

Rosenberg, G., 2006. 'Mångfald som minne och möjlighet', *Arkeologi och mångkultur. Rapport från Svenskt arkeologmöte 2006*, M. Burström (ed.), Södertörns högskola, 11-22.

Schousboe, K., 1989. 'Folketiden – eller da kulturhistorien blev »tidløs«', *Brugte historier. Ti essays om brug og misbrug af historien*, L. Hedeager and K. Schousboe (eds.), København, 165-86.

Selberg, T., 2002. 'Tradisjon, kulturarv og minnespolitikk. Å iscesette, vandre i og fortelle om fortiden', *Historien in på livet*, A. Eriksen, J. Garnet and T. Selberg (eds.), Lund, 9-28.

Stenroth, I., 2005. *Sveriges rötter. En nations födelse*, Lund.

Strömholm, S., 1997. 'Kultur - en gemenskap med inbyggda spänningar', *Tolv kommentarer Om kulturens roll och roller. Kommentarer i anledning av en världskommissions rapport*, B. Göransson (ed.), Stockholm, 11-4.

Sörbom, P., 1998. 'Förord', *Sveriges kulturarv. Att förvalta det förflutna*, U. von Schultz (ed.), Arlöv, 5-6.

Wallette, A., 2004. *Sagans svenskar. Synen på vikingatiden och de isländska sagorna under 300 år*, Malmö.

Årre, K., 1998. 'Svenska museer', *Sveriges kulturarv. Att förvalta det förflutna*, U. von Schultz (ed.), Arlöv, 125-59.

Homepage of the Swedish Museum of National Antiquities; accessed 09-11-2007; http://www.historiska.se/historia/jarnaldern/v ikingar/begreppetvikingar/

Figure 1. The three burial mounds of Old Uppsala, with the medieval church in the background. (Photo by the author).

Figure 2. Viking ship at Edmonton Heritage days. Note the three crowns on a blue field, the national symbol of Sweden, on one of the shields (Photo by K.J. Winberg).

Figure 3. Modern Rune stone in the Swedish archipelago (Photo by the author).

www.ingramcontent.com/pod-product-compliance
Lightning Source LLC
Chambersburg PA
CBHW061004030426
42334CB00033B/3355